GOD'S MUSIC MINISTRY

JAMES EDWARD GOODLETT

JAISHA MINISTRIES LLC

jaishaministries.com

This book is dedicated to my God-given soul mate,
and love of my life, my wife,
Pastor Aisha Goodlett.

TABLE OF CONTENTS

ACKNOWLEDGEMENTS

Special thanks to Bishop Dwight A. Reed and to the great man and woman of God, Christ Apostolic Temple founders Bishop Jeremiah Reed and Mother Willie Mae Reed, my mother Tonya Oliver-McGregor, my brother Ismail Oliver, and my wife, Pastor Aisha Goodlett, all of who's teaching, guidance and love has generated and informed the content of this book. A very special thanks also to Evangelist Kerneater Scott who through her love, generosity, and support has also made this book possible.

FOREWORD

Music has always had the power to move hearts, shift atmospheres, and usher in the very presence of God. It transcends barriers, speaks when words fail, and ministers deeply to the soul. In this book James Goodlett invites us into a deeper understanding of what it truly means to serve in music ministry-not as performers, but as vessels.

It's a special gift when someone you've watched grow up, begins to walk boldly in their God-given calling. That's exactly how I feel about James Goodlett-not just a friend, but more like a nephew to me. Our families had been close for years, I've seen firsthand the heart, humility, and passion he brings to everything he does, especially in the area of music ministry.

This book is a reflection of the life he has pursued in dedication to worshiping, serving and the pursuit of GOD'S presence through music. It's not written from theory, but from a deep desire to see music ministry done to honor God with both excellence and authenticity. In these pages, James pours out wisdom, insight, and encouragement for anyone called to serve through music speaking to the spiritual posture of their heart. He reminds us that music ministry is more than performance- it's a powerful sacred offering that can shift atmospheres, bring healing, and draw people closer to God.

I couldn't be more proud of him, and I'm confident this book will bless many. Whether you're a praise and worship leader, choir member, musician or called to ministry in other areas other than music, there is something here for you. So read with an open heart, and let God speak to you through the wisdom and anointing found in these pages.

With love and admiration,
Pastor Robin Andrews
Resurrected Community Ministries
Louisville, Kentucky

INTRODUCTION

My son, forget not my law; but let thine heart keep my commandments:
For length of days, and long life, and peace, shall they add to thee.
Let not mercy and truth forsake thee: bind them about thy neck; write
them upon the table of thine heart: So shalt thou find favour and good
understanding in the sight of God and man. Trust in the LORD with
all thine heart; and lean not unto thine own understanding. In all thy
ways acknowledge him, and he shall direct thy paths. Be not wise in thine
own eyes: fear the LORD, and depart from evil. It shall be health to thy
navel, and marrow to thy bones. Honour the LORD with thy substance,
and with the firstfruits of all thine increase: So shall thy barns be filled
with plenty, and thy presses shall burst out with new wine.
My son, despise not the chastening of the LORD; neither be weary of his
correction: For whom the LORD loveth he correcteth; even as a father the
son in whom he delighteth. Happy is the man that findeth wisdom, and
the man that getteth understanding. For the merchandise of it is better
than the merchandise of silver, and the gain thereof than fine gold. She
is more precious than rubies: and all the things thou canst desire are not
to be compared unto her. Length of days is in her right hand; and in her
left hand riches and honour. Her ways are ways of pleasantness, and all
her paths are peace. She is a tree of life to them that lay hold upon her:
and happy is every one that retaineth her.

The LORD by wisdom hath founded the earth; by understanding hath he established the heavens. By his knowledge the depths are broken up, and the clouds drop down the dew. My son, let not them depart from thine eyes: keep sound wisdom and discretion: so shall they be life unto thy soul, and grace to thy neck. Then shalt thou walk in thy way safely, and thy foot shall not stumble. When thou liest down, thou shalt not be afraid: yea, thou shalt lie down, and thy sleep shall be sweet. Be not afraid of sudden fear, neither of the desolation of the wicked, when it cometh. For the LORD shall be thy confidence, and shall keep thy foot from being taken. Withhold not good from them to whom it is due, when it is in the power of thine hand to do it. Say not unto thy neighbour, Go, and come again, and to morrow I will give; when thou hast it by thee. Devise not evil against thy neighbour, seeing he dwelleth securely by thee. Strive not with a man without cause, if he have done thee no harm. Envy thou not the oppressor, and choose none of his ways. For the froward is abomination to the LORD: but his secret is with the righteous. The curse of the LORD is in the house of the wicked: but he blesseth the habitation of the just. Surely he scorneth the scorners: but he giveth grace unto the lowly. The wise shall inherit glory: but shame shall be the promotion of fools.

Proverbs 3 KJV

PREFACE

A musician is someone who creates music, yet the process of making music, though diverse in method, ultimately stems from a single source: the vessel. This foundational concept is often overlooked, particularly within the context of music ministry. Whether through information or practice, I deal with how God wants to use us, but we are unaware of what is expected of us. The ministry of music, when aligned with God's purpose, holds profound spiritual power. It communicates deliverance from the flesh and from oppressive spiritual forces. However, when we lack understanding of our true purpose, we tend to interpret life solely through a natural, limited perspective. This disconnect hinders us from fully comprehending the reasons behind our actions and the calling behind our ministry.

We are undoubtedly engaged in a spiritual battle. At the same time, we grapple with our inner selves and the deeper truths that reside within us. Many remain unaware of the existence of the "hidden person of the heart," an inner self that can either lead to our downfall or become the key to our salvation. This lack of awareness often results in individuals unknowingly entering a spiritual state in which they risk falling out of alignment with God.

Poison often masquerades as nourishment, and enemies may present themselves as friends. Such is the nature of evil. It frequently appears in forms that seem desirable. Even those well-versed in biblical teachings can fall victim to deception, as discerning the truth is not always straightforward. To fulfill our roles in music ministry, we must be individuals who walk by faith. Yet, how can we truly walk by faith without cultivating a spiritual perspective?

The music ministry carries significant influence, and many prominent figures have risen to positions of considerable power within it. However, a lack of accountability has resulted in substantial harm being carried out under the guise of serving the Lord, often fueled more by fleshly ambition than by genuine spiritual calling.

The absence of spiritual principles in an individual inevitably leads to the distortion of their ministry. The widespread deterioration of the music ministry has caused deep harm, turning the hearts of entire generations away from the church. Sexual immorality, self-exaltation, and the relentless pursuit of pleasure have infiltrated this sacred space, resulting in many musicians, singers, worshippers, ministers, preachers, and even high-ranking clergy living in ways that contradict the teachings of God. Rather than serving as a place of refuge and spiritual restoration, the church has, in many cases, devolved into a stage for carnal expression and superficial performance. Within this environment, individuals often compete for power, influence, and relationships, blind to the reality that they have yielded themselves to the enemy, whose mission is to undermine and ultimately destroy the church.

The music ministry within the church is facing profound challenges, yet many remain unaware of the severity of the situation. Those who do recognize it often lack the spiritual strength or resolve to make transformative decisions that could preserve their spiritual well-being. As a result, a cycle emerges in which individuals attempt to live beyond their spiritual means, repeatedly falling into the same destructive patterns. While some earnestly seek deliverance, they struggle to experience lasting progress. This raises a critical question: what can be done?

After years of failure, trial and error, dedicated study, and the guidance of my pastor, I have come to understand the true purpose of the music ministry. This book seeks to preserve and impart the foundational principles of God's design for music ministry, offering direction for those seeking to align their service with His will. It is essential that we not only know but fully comprehend what God expects of us, so that we may effectively fulfill the mission of the church.

The primary purpose of the Church is to lead souls to salvation. Yet how can this mission be accomplished if we operate based on feelings, personal opinions, and sporadic moments of inspiration, rather than maintaining a consistent focus on God's divine purpose for us? How can we truly fulfill our life's calling while living in self-deception and misleading others about what it means to serve God? Though we profess to worship Him, our hearts are often clouded by competing intentions and misguided priorities.

On Father's Day, my pastor, Bishop Jeremiah Reed, posed a profound Question: *"Who is your father?"* The influence of music can sometimes tempt us to elevate ourselves, reflecting the prideful nature of our fleshly father: *Satan*. Many of us fall into disobedience, mistakenly believing that God does not see us simply because He is not physically visible. According to *John 3:3-5* and *Acts 2:38*, being baptized in Jesus' name and filled with the Holy Ghost qualifies us for the kingdom, but it does not guarantee our entry. We must continually battle the flesh and strive to fulfill God's will in our lives. Though many have experienced the initial steps of salvation, they remain entangled in personal struggles and time is not always on their side. Ultimately, obedience is essential to our salvation.

The weight of sharing these reflections has been heavy on my heart, as I, too, have faced numerous challenges both personally and within the music ministry. Were it not for the steadfast support of my pastor, I might not have had the strength to continue. As human beings born into sin, we nonetheless possess the extraordinary opportunity to operate in a high and holy capacity, fulfilling one of the greatest purposes ever entrusted to humanity by God. God's expectations are high, and the responsibilities of the music ministry must be approached with deep reverence and intentionality. My aim is to be thought-provoking in my approach, encouraging not only reflection but also action, prompting you to ask difficult questions and engage in meaningful research. Some concepts are intentionally presented as redundant and open-ended, inviting you to uncover deeper truths through personal study and meditation. My hope is that many will give careful attention to these principles, embracing them as I have, so that they may be blessed, fulfill their divine purpose, and ultimately offer a life story that is pleasing to God.

CHAPTER ONE
THE VESSEL

So God created man in His own image, in the image of God created He him; male and female created He them. And God blessed them, and God said unto them, Be fruitful, and multiply, and replenish the earth, and subdue it: and have dominion over the fish of the sea, and over the foul of the air, and over every living thing that moveth upon the earth.

Genesis 1:27-28 KJV

I beseech you therefore, brethren, by the mercies of God, that ye present your bodies a living sacrifice, holy, acceptable unto God, which is your reasonable service. And be not conformed to this world: but be ye transformed by the renewing of your mind, that ye may prove what is that good, and acceptable, and perfect, will of God.

Romans 12:1-2 KJV

Know ye not that ye are the temple of God, and that the Spirit of God dwelleth in you? If any man defile the temple of God, him shall God destroy; for the temple of God is holy, which temple ye are.

1 Corinthians 3:16-17 KJV

The Temple

The heart, our body's tireless engine, pumps life-sustaining blood through an intricate network of vessels, delivering vital nutrients and oxygen while carrying away harmful waste. Yet, despite its remarkable resilience, the heart remains vulnerable. Heart disease stands as the leading cause of death today, most often stemming from damage that hinders its ability to function properly. Contributing factors such as unhealthy diets, sedentary lifestyles, and inherited risks can silently erode heart health over time. When the heart fails, life itself becomes unsustainable. Close behind, stroke ranks as the second leading cause of death, occurring when blood flow to the brain is suddenly blocked. This deprivation of oxygen can cause irreversible brain damage, or prove fatal.

The human body is susceptible to a host of afflictions, cancer, diabetes, and countless others that threaten its vitality. Yet, in the beginning, the story was vastly different. When God created man, He crafted a perfect vessel, one infused with divine breath, becoming a living soul. Woman was created in like perfection, and together they dwelled in the sacred garden of God, whole and unbroken, until they chose to disregard His command.

Humanity was designed not merely to exist, but to carry out God's will on earth. Man bore the responsibility of imparting God's word and guiding his wife in that truth, fully aware of the grave consequences that would follow disobedience. The moment that divine relationship was fractured, death entered the human experience, and with it came the curse, sickness, suffering, and the many diseases that plague the body today.

Yet even now, the core purpose of humanity endures: we are meant to be vessels of God's work. A vessel, in itself, holds no power. Its significance lies in the purpose it serves and the power it is given to fulfill that purpose.

It's widely accepted that we tap into only a fraction of our brain's true potential, yet even that small portion has fueled some of the most extraordinary achievements in human history. As the global population has surged, so too has the complexity of our lives. We remain captivated by the ingenuity of ancient civilizations, even as we stand in a modern world overflowing with knowledge, instantly accessible, always within reach.

With a swipe or a click, we can explore nearly any subject, uncover lost histories, and master new skills. Yet, amid this unprecedented access to information, we often fail to pause and consider the weight of such privilege. This unexamined abundance may help explain why so many who claim faith in God find themselves struggling to walk fully in their calling despite being under the spiritual care of pastors appointed to guide and equip them. Without reflection, even divine instruction can fall on inattentive minds.

When reflecting on your relationship with God, have you ever truly considered your body, your very being before Him? Have you taken time to ponder the extraordinary gift of life He's entrusted to you, along with the weighty responsibility that comes with it? Have you sought the answer to that timeless question: *What is my purpose?*

The word offers a clear response. In the King James Version, the Bible declares that the whole duty of man is to "fear God and keep His commandments." Within that calling, each of us is uniquely gifted, endowed with inherent abilities and the capacity to develop talents that reflect both our nature and God's direction for our lives.

But how often do we truly pause to consider the broader scope of God's work and our individual role within it? What are your priorities? And do they align with the purpose for which you were created?

The body is a remarkable network of interdependent systems, working in harmony to form the soul-the total person, a unified expression of mind, body, and spirit. As we navigate life, our choices and behaviors, whether wise or reckless, inevitably shape our overall well-being.

In a time when awareness of physical and mental health is on the rise, many express appreciation for the shift toward healthier living. But how many of us truly acknowledge, let alone prioritize, the spiritual dimension of our health? It's often the most overlooked, yet arguably the most essential, aspect of what it means to be whole.

In the epistles, we are reminded that we are the temple of God and that His Spirit dwells within us. Yet this indwelling occurs in bodies that are constantly aging, fragile and finite. Our daily choices reflect the path we walk, and it is the *condition* of our hearts that ultimately shapes those decisions.

That's why our minds must be in alignment with God's purpose, and our bodies, His sacred vessels, must be yielded to His will. We must never lose sight of this truth: we have been bought with a price.

So the question stands, not only for reflection but for action: Are you a faithful steward of the Lord's temple?

<u>Food</u>

Let's be honest, food is fun. It's woven into nearly every meaningful moment in life: church gatherings, funerals, celebrations, family milestones. Show up to an event without food, and you'll quickly feel the void. Food is more than nourishment; it's deeply tied to our emotions, psychological well-being, and for many, even our spirituality. It embodies life, culture, and connection. Yet in today's society, our relationship with food has grown increasingly problematic.

There are approximately 10,000 taste buds on your tongue, each responsible for detecting different flavors. Bitter tastes are sensed on the back of the tongue, sour at the sides, umami in the center, salty toward the front, and sweet at the tip. But here's the twist, most of what we perceive as taste is actually smell. Taste is a complex neurological event in which the brain interprets signals from both the nose and the tongue. And behind much of what we "taste" lies a powerful industry few truly consider.

Enter the world of synthetic flavoring. If you've never heard of a "taste factory," now you have. These places engineer thousands of chemicals to replicate flavors we crave, labeling them vaguely as "natural flavor" or "artificial flavor" on packaging. Two must-read books, *Salt Sugar Fat* by Michael Moss and *The Dorito Effect* by Mark Schatzker, unpack how food giants have strategically manipulated our palates for profit. What's worse, the FDA doesn't always fully regulate or even understand these practices.

We often joke about "junk food," yet the term is revealing. We wouldn't keep literal junk in our homes, yet we consume it daily. Many of these foods offer virtually no nutritional value and are loaded with chemicals that serve no beneficial purpose to the human body. What's more troubling is this manipulation extends beyond taste factories; many food manufacturers worldwide are also adding ingredients to stimulate appetite, leading to patterns of overconsumption.

Processed foods, found in nearly every grocery aisle, are known to contribute to cognitive decline, hormonal imbalance, and chronic illness. On top of that, we're ingesting microplastics and synthetic chemicals that have infiltrated our bodies, including our brains. These substances interfere with cellular function and immune response, increasing the risk of disease, including cancer. Alarmingly, many of the ingredients allowed in American food products are banned in other countries due to their harmful effects.

From a biblical perspective, we have some idea of the foods Adam and Eve consumed, pure, natural, and life-giving. Though Adam's disobedience ushered in death, we are still capable of drawing health and strength from what God created. Unfortunately, the rise of pharmaceutical industries has promoted synthetic "solutions" for conditions often caused by poor dietary choices. As Steve Jobs once said, *"Eat your food as medicine, otherwise you will have to eat medicine as your food."*

This isn't to demonize the entire medical community, I have doctors and nurses in my own family, but from personal experience and observation, I've seen the burnout and apathy that often emerge within the system. Healthcare has become entangled in politics, insurance, and corporate interests. Tragically, death itself has become profitable.

Consider how diet directly impacts how our bodies manage carbohydrates. When we eat carbs, they're broken down into glucose, our main energy source. That glucose enters the bloodstream, prompting the pancreas to release insulin, which ushers the glucose into cells. But high sucrose intake can dull the body's sensitivity to glucose. When the body fails to detect glucose altogether, it will not release insulin. This is Type 1 diabetes. When the body produces insufficient insulin or can't use it effectively, this is Type 2 diabetes. Both conditions contribute to complications like heart disease.

"Garbage in, garbage out." This isn't just a saying, it's a sobering truth that affects our health, our clarity, and the very temple of God. I'm not here to tell you to eliminate every indulgence. But as people

called to serve the Lord, we should be thoughtful stewards of our bodies.

Our bodies are not just instruments, they are the vessels through which our ministry flows. While instruments can be tuned and replaced, the body is the source from which our music, our service, and our impact resonate. The more intentionally we care for it, the more powerfully we can fulfill our calling.

Exercise And Occupation

A healthy diet is undeniably important, but we must not underestimate the transformative power of regular exercise. Staying physically active is one of the most effective ways to preserve health, slow the aging process, and enhance mental sharpness. Beyond the physical, it cultivates a sense of vitality and emotional well-being.

Consider walking: it supports cardiovascular health, aids in weight management, and clears the mind. Running, on the other hand, has been shown to improve sleep and elevate mood. Swimming, cycling, and strength training not only build endurance and muscle, but can also improve sexual health and confidence. These are just a few examples, yet each contributes to improved mental clarity, emotional balance, and overall wellness.

But wellness extends beyond diet and exercise, it also includes the impact of our careers. The work we do daily can either support or hinder our physical health. For instance, a keyboardist or guitarist, who chooses a physically demanding job like construction may risk injuring their hands, potentially jeopardizing their craft. A physical education teacher, with constant vocal use, may strain their voice. And careers requiring repetitive lifting, such as warehouse work, can take a serious toll on joints and the spine, particularly for drummers or those whose work relies on physical precision.

It's essential to evaluate how our occupational choices and lifestyle habits affect our bodies. This includes often-overlooked areas such as sleep, stress management, rest, and mental health, all of which play a role in how prepared we are to fulfill our calling.

Our bodies are not just biological machines, they are temples, sacred vessels entrusted with God's work. To maintain them, we must approach life with intention: a clear vision, a well-structured plan, measurable goals, daily discipline, and unwavering commitment. Living well is not simply about adding years to your life. It's about adding life to your years, all in service of a higher purpose.

The Spiritual Man

The heart is the problem. Not the organ that beats in our chest, but the inner core of our being, what the Bible refers to in *Jeremiah 17:9*. This is the essence of our fallen nature: a human nature driven by desires that is desperate to fight God in every way. This is spiritual heart disease.

Just as physical health depends on what we consume, our spiritual health is shaped by our spiritual diet. Even after salvation, sanctification is an ongoing process, one marked by daily decisions, internal battles, and the constant question: *Will I obey God today?*

Obedience is not passive. God requires active participation in His kingdom, and that participation is worship. True prosperity, spiritual prosperity, is found only in walking according to His commandments. It may not always match our worldly expectations, but It's the only path that leads to life and peace.

Saying something untrue is lying, but so is living in contradiction to God's truth. How can we minister through music while living outside His principles? Too often, we overlook basic commands, like giving tithes and offerings, an act required of all, including leaders. Neglecting this places us under a curse. Every one in the music ministry should always bring their method of payment if not online. It's time to look inward and ask God to uncover what lies beneath the surface. If God is seeking *true worshippers*, there must also be impostors, and many may be found in the music ministry.

As we delve deeper into God's calling through music, we must not lose sight of who we are, or who we were. This is not a casual calling. Ministry, especially through music, is sacred and carries weight. Many who have handled this calling lightly have paid a devastating price. The church today finds itself in a fragile state, drifting from God and entangled in performance and self-promotion. Titles have become trophies, and many ministers have exchanged calling for personal gain.

Meanwhile, the true enemy operates freely among us, unrecognized and unchallenged. This is not just a concern; it's a crisis. Spiritual warfare is real. Demonic forces, far older and more experienced than we are, understand the power of music better than much of the modern church. Ask yourself: *Who was the first minister of music?* The answer reveals just how seriously the enemy takes this realm. And make no mistake, the devil always comes to church. This is about far more than emotion or artistry. This is about souls.

It's time we believe and live the songs we sing. God makes extraordinary moves, but His ways are not our ways. The root of sin is unbelief. Many doubt God because they don't know Him. If we truly understood who He is, believing in His goodness, provision, and desire for our wholeness would come naturally. He wants us to live fulfilled, purposeful, prosperous lives, physically, spiritually, emotionally. He desires that we be whole, that we find companionship aligned with our purpose, and that we walk in divine health, for our bodies are His temple.

Yes, He is a righteous judge, a "terrible God" in the biblical sense of awe-inspiring power, but this does not mean we live in terror. It means that safety is found in obedience. Flourishing follows faithfulness. Get to know God, pray without ceasing, reflect deeply, and learn through your experiences. There's so much the enemy wants to keep you from discovering. Fight back by growing in your knowledge of God.

A fruitless ministry begins with unbelief. If you are to lead others, you must be the first to believe.

Music ministry has the power to heal. God cares about our health, body and soul. There are moments in worship when words fall away, and music alone becomes the ministry. I've experienced this. In those moments, healing flows not from us, but through us. That is what the world must see in us: not performance, but spiritual power. Not talent, but testimony.

This calling demands more than sound, it demands sanctification. Not performance, but perseverance. God will carry you through the trials, and each one will shape and elevate you. Others may depend on your gifts, but God is trusting you with this ministry.

That's why He placed it in your hands. Because you are not just playing notes or singing melodies. You are carrying His message. You are His vessel.

Chapter Two

ADVERSARY

Put on the whole armour of God, that ye may be able to stand against the wiles of the devil. For we wrestle not against flesh and blood, but against spiritual wickedness in high places.
Ephesians 6:11-12 KJV

Let not sin reign in your mortal body, that ye should obey it in the lusts thereof. Neither yield ye your members as instruments of unrighteousness unto sin: but yield ye yourselves unto God, as those that are alive from the dead, and your members as instruments of righteousness unto God.
Romans 6:12-13 KJV

But when he saw Jesus afar off, he ran and worshipped him, And cried with a loud voice, and said, What have I to do with thee, Jesus, thou Son of the most high God? I adjure thee by God, that thou torment me not. For he said unto him, Come out of the man, thou unclean spirit. And he asked him, What is thy name? And he answered, saying, My name is Legion: for we are many. And he besought him much that he would not send them away out of the country. Now there was there nigh unto the mountains a great herd of swine feeding. And all the devils besought him, saying, Send us into the swine, that we may enter into them. And forthwith Jesus gave them leave. And the unclean spirits went out, and entered into the swine: and the herd ran violently down a steep place into the sea, (they were about two thousand;) and were choked in the sea. And they that fed the swine fled, and told it in the city, and in the country. And they went out to see what it was that was done. And they come to Jesus, and see him that was possessed with the devil, and had the legion, sitting, and clothed, and in his right mind: and they were afraid.

Mark 5:6-15 KJV

Preparation

The world is in turmoil over what we commonly call climate change. Thunderstorms, hurricanes, tornadoes, and wildfires are growing in both intensity and frequency, bringing with them devastating financial burdens and posing grave threats to human life. The disruption of once-stable environmental patterns has shaken communities around the globe. In response, society is being forced to pivot, to prepare, adapt, and brace for what's next. Preparation is key to overcoming these challenges. Similarly, by putting on the whole armor of God, we are preparing for the inevitable, an attack.

What is amiss to many of the Christian faith is that living for Christ is a spiritual walk. This is not about the natural way of life although your spiritual life must be the foundation of your natural life. In living this spiritual life your walk is determined by your faith and your faith must be in truth. To walk in truth, you must first receive truth, and that truth is revealed to you through divine revelation. Through revelation, you come to understand that while the Bible as a whole is not the word of God, the word of God can be found within it.

We are most familiar with the King James Version of the Bible, which was based on the canonization of the Dead Sea Scrolls commissioned By King James I of England. Seven years his scholars toiled to produce this work which was a stunt for the peasant folk to recognize their king had produced the true bible to help solidify his influence. While several manuscripts were used in this process, others were omitted or altered, and translation is not always an exact science.

History, after all, is a record shaped by the needs, biases, and limitations of its time. What spoke to one generation may not fully resonate with another. Thus, it becomes imperative that we study scripture with discernment, seeking context, questioning assumptions, and earnestly asking: what is truly the word of God?

The Fallen One

"Helel" is the original Hebrew term meaning *"shining one"* or *"bringer of light."* In the book of *Isaiah*, this word was later rendered in Latin as *"Lucifer,"* a name that, over time, became deeply associated with the figure now known as Satan, *the adversary*. In *Revelation*, he is also referred to as *the dragon, that old serpent,* among other epithets. While the Bible and tradition offer a host of descriptions, it remains possible that his original name is lost to us. For the purposes of this discourse, I will use the terms *Lucifer* and *Satan* interchangeably.

Lucifer has long been a figure of fascination, his story woven through myth, folklore, and theology alike. Tradition holds that he was a Seraphim, chosen from the angelic choir and elevated to the role of prince over the host. Biblically, he is described as *"the anointed cherub that covereth,"* adorned with every precious stone, perfect in form and radiant in beauty, exceptional, even by celestial standards. The text speaks of his tabrets and pipes, a reference many interpret as musical instrumentation, suggesting a sacred role in musical worship. Positioned upon the holy mountain of God, covering the very throne of God, Lucifer was a being of exalted status, a celestial luminary and clearly very influential.

Many believe he was heaven's minister of music, the conductor of divine praise. But as the word tells us, it was pride that corrupted him. He leveraged his charm, beauty, and persuasive power to draw quite a few of the angelic host into rebellion. Lucifer won the support of a third, but I'm willing to believe he visited as many as he could to sell his agenda. The sheer gravity of that reality should give us pause.

Now consider this: God, omniscient, omnipresent, omnipotent, allowed it to happen. He watched as Lucifer went from angel to angel, spreading his deception, sowing discord in paradise. And yet, from what we can tell, God did not immediately intervene. He allowed events to unfold, a war to erupt in the perfect splendor of heaven itself. Only afterward were Lucifer and his followers cast out. If war could break out in the presence of God, in heaven, how can we, in our broken and fallen world, expect life to be free from conflict, even within the church?

Let us examine the *spirit of Satan.* According to the word of God, Lucifer was intoxicated by self-ambition. A created being, he somehow believed he could ascend above his Creator and seize dominion over all. Referred to by Jesus as *"the father of lies,"* Satan embodies deception. His persuasive power was so profound that he drew a third of heaven's angels into his rebellion. And this is key: the enemy rarely presents himself as evil. He does not appear grotesque but desirable, offering what appears beneficial, enlightened, and liberating. He packages temptation in subtlety, in charm, and in reasonableness. His goal? To convince us there is something more appealing, more satisfying, more true than what God has already declared.

Distraction is another of his chief tactics. While blatant evil is often recognizable, the more dangerous deceptions and distractions come clothed in the appearance of good. Even Scripture can be manipulated to serve the enemy's purpose, as we saw in his temptation of Christ. Without discernment, we risk mistaking compromise for conviction, believing we are walking with God when in fact, we are wandering toward destruction. Some things are purposefully made complicated to hide and distort truth.

Furthermore, when it comes to personal character, we can become intoxicated with our own self-image, developing a natural tendency to cling to our own perspectives even when they stand in opposition to the truth.

It's important to understand: Satan is not omnipresent. He is one spirit, and can only be in one place at a time. So, when you feel as if "the devil is on your track, trying to turn you back," it's likely not Satan himself, but one of many adversarial spirits operating under his command. Yet those sealed by the Holy Ghost need not fear. The real question is not whether the enemy is tempting you, but whether you will yield to that temptation.

Eve was deceived, yes, but she *chose*. That choice is at the heart of the matter. Did the devil "made" you do it? Hold that thought! I am not simply discussing demonic influence, I am dealing with the power of decision. People may be influenced, even enticed, but they remain accountable for the choices they make. If the just must live by faith, then they must also live with the conviction that God is sovereign, that He holds the world in His hands and that all reality unfolds according to His divine order.

Spiritual Integrity

Far too often, we unknowingly partner with the enemy, not because we desire evil, but because we believe God should have acted differently. When divine decisions clash with human expectations, disillusionment sets in. Yet the truth remains: a gift belongs to God. It's entrusted to individuals for the purpose of ministry, not for validation by others. Jealousy and envy, however, run rampant in the church. Favor is not always fair, and those consumed by resentment risk undermining their own calling by obsessing over the perceived unworthiness of others.

Many who claim the name of Christ spend more time critiquing the spiritual standing of others than cultivating their own character, blind to the reality that they themselves may be out of alignment with God. Yes, God is love, but His statutes are the evidence of that love. If the terms *mote* and *beam* mean nothing to you, take a moment to revisit the book of *Matthew*. If you've been wounded, don't live in the realm of imagination, go directly to the source and pursue truth.

Worship is not confined to a song or a service. It is a life in complete submission to the creative order of God. When your life is governed by His principles, you are living under the rule of the Kingdom. And in any kingdom, it is the king who decides, not the citizens. God distributes gifts according to His will, not ours.

Talents and abilities are meant to glorify God, not elevate self. Throughout history, those who exalted themselves have been humbled by the hand of God. If our lives are but a vapor, here today and gone tomorrow, what becomes of our accountability? God sees beyond appearances, He knows our motives, our intentions, our every thought. We are fragile beings, subject to death at any moment. What we think we own can vanish in an instant. Do not be deceived.

In today's church culture, production and entertainment often masquerade as ministry. The line between the club and the sanctuary has grown faint in the minds of many. Music ministries that once ushered in the presence of God now mirror the world's stage performances. There must be a clear distinction between what is sacred and what is secular. When that distinction is lost, someone has lost their light. We deceive ourselves into thinking God will accept whatever we offer simply because our intentions are good. We assume that appealing to culture, especially youth culture, under the guise of outreach, is enough to earn God's approval.

But many are "doing church" without God. They confuse emotional highs with divine encounters, believing the presence of emotion means the presence of anointing. Yet emotional experiences are not exclusive to sanctuaries, people feel deeply moved in strip clubs and concerts, too. If God is truly King, then what do we actually have to offer Him? Consider Cain, when his offering fell short, he responded with violence. What, then, is the true purpose of church?

If you are part of the Church of the Living God, you are part of a spiritual war. And the opposition will stop at nothing to sabotage, infiltrate, and dismantle ministries in any way possible, especially from within. You will face adversity, even possibly threats to your life. This is still the same world where Christians were once martyred for sport, and where believers are still dying today for the name of Jesus. Make no mistake: this is war. In war, a soldier does not negotiate. They obey orders.

A music ministry that is truly aligned with God's will brings transformation and healing, and the kingdom of darkness will respond with attacks on unity, leadership, and purpose. Leaders in the music ministry must be especially vigilant. Spiritual warfare will target them, because music has power to influence minds, shape atmospheres, and shift hearts. Those in leadership must develop discernment, to recognize not only the enemy, but the subtle ways in which he infiltrates. Preventive structure is not optional; It's essential. Clear expectations and boundaries must be established to protect the integrity of the ministry.

If the music ministry is not united in purpose and aligned with God's vision, it will fall short of what God designed. Getting the mind of God is not a suggestion, it is a necessity. He knows what He wants. Only when we hear Him clearly can we carry out His will with integrity and excellence. Authority within the ministry must be respected, exercised justly, and honored mutually. And the invisible undercurrents, the unresolved tensions and unspoken offenses, must be addressed. They erode trust and weaken the body. Don't live in speculation or assumption. Go to the source. Seek truth from both parties and witnesses.

It's easy to get tangled in petty disputes. Insecurity has a way of magnifying trivial issues into major conflicts. But wisdom teaches us to choose our battles. Not every disagreement warrants confrontation. Usually addressing root principles resolves surface problems. Discern what's eternal from what's temporary. Handle real matters in the right time and place, and let the rest go.

Keep the broader mission in view. Don't waste your strength harming people who may not know how to do better. If someone wrongs you, be the bigger person. Develop spiritual endurance. Be patient. Show love. Pray. Release offenses. It's not worth carrying. In the grand scheme of things, many of these burdens don't matter. What matters is that God is still on the throne, and it was never about us to begin with.

Spiritual Forces

When a person comes under the influence of a spiritual force, they may begin to lose control over aspects of their will, especially in areas governed by that spirit. Their actions, decisions, and even thoughts may no longer reflect their true character. In extreme cases, the consequences are devastating, people have lost marriages, families, and even their lives due to entanglement with malevolent spiritual forces. Acts of violence, including murder and suicide, are sometimes rooted not in psychological causes alone but in spiritual oppression. The spiritual realm is both real and perilous, and its influence should never be underestimated.

More sobering still is the reality that individuals, especially those in positions of leadership—can transmit the spiritual conditions they carry to others. Whether knowingly or not, they extend their spiritual atmosphere to those around them, amplifying both light or darkness in the lives they touch.

This becomes particularly evident when a person's behavior begins to shift after close association with certain individuals. We often think we know people well, but true understanding requires both time and discernment. Many lack the ability to read character deeply, missing the subtle cues and patterns that expose the reality beneath the surface.

Spiritual maladies, like physical diseases, can be contagious. Association with the wrong individuals, particularly those whose spiritual disposition is contrary to God, can corrupt your own spirit. At times, even physical contact can be dangerous. In Jesus's parable, the "fowls of the air" represent demonic forces, including people, that come to destroy what was planted. We assume we know our neighbors, but this assumption can be fatal. Forming close relationships indiscriminately, even within the church, can expose us to spiritual harm. Jesus also warned of tares sown among the wheat, illustrating that not all who appear to belong to God truly do. And tragically, when some fall away from the faith, they often take others down with them. Also take special notice of *Matthew 15:14*.

When God speaks, His word is final. Entertaining debate or inviting outside opinions on what God has personally instructed you to do can open the door to confusion, compromise, and eventual disobedience. What God gives you is uniquely yours. Others may not fully grasp its weight or purpose. To protect your spiritual clarity, it is sometimes necessary to step away from voices that distract from what God has spoken.

This is why leadership is such a sacred and serious responsibility. One of the core truths of spiritual leadership is that a leader's spirit inevitably influences those under their authority. Their attitudes, values, and behaviors, whether healthy or toxic, are transferred. Leaders must lead with humility, discernment, and spiritual integrity, aware that what flows from them shapes the people around them.

Geography also plays a role in spiritual warfare. Certain regions are marked by chaos, confusion, and violence, manifestations of demonic influence over the land. For instance, there was once a house in Wisconsin, now demolished, where few who entered ever returned alive. Some places are gateways into the spiritual realm, where people have reportedly encountered beings they believed were human, but were not. There are areas in the sea where aircraft and ships disappear, locations even wildlife instinctively avoids. My wife and several companions once drove through a wooded area early one morning, where they witnessed people amongst the trees. An overwhelming presence of death surrounded them, and moments later, the people were gone. These are not mere tales, they are warnings. Too many who enter such places out of curiosity never make it back. Not all missing persons are the result of human activity.

Our environment has a profound influence on our spirit. This is why mentorship matters: if you want to build wealth, spend time with those who have. Spiritually, the same principle applies. True leaders are not shaped by crowds, they shape the environment around them. They possess a discernment that pierces beyond surface impressions. They don't seek validation from people. Instead, they move according to divine direction. Yet even the strongest are not immune to spiritual attack.

Human beings are born vessels, designed to be filled. But because we are born under the curse of sin, we are also vulnerable to spiritual possession. When an evil spirit gains access, it can assume control of a person's behavior. In all my years, I've never met anyone named Judas. Names carry weight. Those who lack spiritual discernment are easy targets for the enemy's schemes. This lack of awareness may explain how many churches have begun to embrace ideologies, such as the normalization of homosexuality and lesbianism, that stray from God's original design.

We often quote the phrase "the enemy comes in like a flood," but few understand how systematic his strategies are. With the knowledge and experience from heaven, the enemy has studied humanity for generations, learning how to subtly turn hearts from God. Many believers, lacking skill in spiritual warfare, have lost their zeal, their discernment, and in some cases, their spiritual lives, though they may still attend church, shout, or speak in tongues. The deception is so advanced that some have been unknowingly recruited into the enemy's army, working against the very kingdom they claim to serve.

So when we sing, *"I'm a soldier in the army of the Lord,"* we must pause and ask: which *lord* do we serve? The word "lord" simply means one who has authority over you. If that authority isn't God, then whom are you truly serving?

Salvation is deliverance-from sin, from spiritual bondage, from the grip of the enemy-and no one can hold your past against you. But many misunderstand even foundational spiritual truths. For instance, speaking in tongues is often misrepresented. The word "tongue" means language. When God gives someone the gift of tongues, it is to communicate the Gospel in a real language to people who would not otherwise understand. No human can speak multiple heavenly languages at once. This is a supernatural act only God can perform. The infilling of the Holy Ghost is God Himself entering the vessel of a human being, enabling them to live a spiritual life. It is His seal, His down payment, of the eternal promise to come. And the initial evidence of this infilling is an audible sound. Because believers are priests before God, some may receive a special grace to communicate with Him in divine language. Read *1 Corinthians 14:4*. But always, the source is God, not human.

Warfare

Attacks often come from within, and this truth must not be overlooked or dismissed. While strong family ties are a blessing, they can also become the source of some of life's most painful and disorienting opposition. To endure such moments, one must be spiritually grounded and mentally fortified. In *Matthew 10:34-39*, Jesus offers a sobering perspective on the cost of true discipleship: following Him may demand separation from even our most cherished relationships. Conflict can arise between parent and child, husband and wife, sibling and friend.

I know this reality firsthand. There came a time when I had to place my devotion to God above my relationship with my wife at the time, and even my children, a heart-wrenching decision, yet one necessary for obedience. The question remains: are you truly strong enough to surrender *everything* for God? Many profess they would. But words spoken in comfort often fall silent in the heat of sacrifice. The real test isn't in what we say, it's in what we're willing to lay down when the moment comes.

You may feel burdened by life's challenges, and *Job 14:1* certainly affirms that human life is fraught with trouble. However, when you become actively engaged in God's work, the intensity of spiritual warfare escalates. The more you do for the Kingdom, the greater a threat you pose to the enemy and thus, the more frequent and severe the attacks.

Leaders are prime targets. If the enemy can bring down a leader, he destabilizes the entire organization beneath them. One fallen leader can cause a ripple effect of confusion, discouragement, and collapse. That's why leaders endure some of the most relentless spiritual warfare because they pose the greatest threat to the forces of darkness. The Christian walk is not for the faint of heart. It is a narrow road paved with sacrifice, shaped by trials, and sustained by unwavering commitment.

Question: *Where do all the problems come from in the church?*

Answer: *Saints operating in darkness, working in their flesh in collaboration with demonic forces.*

These aren't always the ones on the fringes. You'll find them front and center, singing songs, directing choirs, praise teams, and playing instruments. The enemy has infiltrated many music ministries with subtle but destructive influence. Iniquity is a *condition*. The result? A church that, in many cases, mirrors the world so closely that the lines between the sacred and the secular are nearly invisible.

I once saw a post online where a woman, enamored with the musical atmosphere of the venue, asked, "What club is this?" The man replied, "It's not a club. It's church."

CHAPTER THREE

THE HEART

For out of the heart proceed evil thoughts, murders, adulteries, fornica-
tions, thefts, false witness, blasphemies: These are the things which defile
a man: but to eat with unwashen hands defileth not a man.
Matthew 15:19-20 KJV

As a man thinketh in his heart, so his he...
Proverbs 23:7 KJV

But the LORD said unto Samuel, Look not on his countenance, or on the
height of his stature; because I have refused him: for the LORD seeth
not as man seeth; for man looketh on the outward appearance, but the
LORD looketh on the heart.
1 Samuel 16:7 KJV

Belief

For generations, we have sung songs proclaiming that we are in the
army of the Lord. Yet, spiritual mortality remains alarmingly high,

with even pastors and other supposed spiritual leaders falling prey to Satanic influences. These individuals may not explicitly worship Satan, but their unbelief is evident. Unbelief is the greatest sin and the most significant form of satanic influence, as demonstrated by the fall of Adam and Eve. Our attitudes toward God have shifted, thus our behavior. We have caused many to lose their faith because they were depending on us. We no longer truly believe the songs we sing, nor do we fully understand their meaning.

Your heart is the core of your being; it is the seat of your will and the control center of your life. The true essence of who you really are resides in your heart, and many of you that are reading this may still need to meet yourself. This is the operational shadow person in you that has deceived you into thinking you are someone or something else. This is the one God seeks to transform. This transformation is the purpose of the preached word which biblically, people think it foolish. Your paradigm must be altered.

A pure heart produces a pure vessel, and we must protect our minds from harmful influences. We all can see society around us and how desperate it is to fulfill the lusts of the flesh in and out of church. Power-hungry individuals have exacerbated political theater, crushed people in the entertainment industry, and destroyed lives within the church. Many are consumed by the pursuit of pleasure with little regard for the consequences, while children are left confused by the actions of so-called role models. The minds of people today are under intense pressure.

Mental health is not secondary, it is central. Losing your mind is not simply about memory; it's about identity. When you can no longer recognize people, when anxiety clouds every decision, when thoughts become disjointed or reality seems to unravel, you are not just struggling, you are unraveling. Your mind is *you*. And once the mind is compromised, so is your life.

Transformation begins with exposure. If you want to change your thinking, you must first change your environment. Growth is impossible in toxic soil. You cannot flourish while remaining rooted in what poisons you. If you are sacred, then your conduct must reflect that truth. If you are the temple of the living God, regardless of how unworthy you may feel, then by His designation, you are holy.

Belief is not just knowing a bit of information. It is an idea you are invested in. Revisit that faithless line. Can you please God without faith? If not, why is it so prevalent among those who claim to love God? This is why I say that we neither believe what we sing nor fully understand it. If we sing songs about doing all things through Christ and that all things work together for good, why is there so much division among us? Why so much distrust, stress, and disrespect? Why do we harbor negative attitudes toward our neighbors instead of showing love? How did the enemy gain such influence over us, especially when the Creator lives within us? How did we end up with people in the music ministry who do not truly believe? What, then, is the true purpose of the church?

Fear is an emotion, typically arising from the belief that someone or something poses a threat or that a negative outcome is imminent. If you do nothing, nothing will happen. If you do something, something will happen. Talking is one thing. Doing is another. The most effective way to overcome fear is to confront it directly. Not knowing how to do something is a poor excuse not to do it. People invest significant time and money to acquire knowledge, and you have already learned how to navigate life up to this point.

A movie I saw expressed how fear kills the mind. I also saw a post online that we are born with two types of fear, the fear of falling and the fear of loud noises. It went on to say all other fear is learned in life.

The fear of God refers to a deep reverence and respect for Him in the knowledge that all God's ways are judgment. He is a God of standards and principles and you must live a righteous life to please Him. In contrast, fear rooted in doubt will hinder one's spiritual success. Many individuals have gotten in trouble with God because they allowed fear to override obedience. When God speaks and you respond with obedience, success will follow.

Sight

A Christian should live with the concept of divorcing themselves from that which is tangible. We understand that which we know but many of us don't know God. Understanding the Christian life is to live in the knowledge of our relationship to God. Emotions, feelings, and reasoning must be positioned last as our judgment should hinge on the substance matter of reality. Imagination is a big reason why saints live in doubt. If God said it, there is nothing else. If Adam and Eve would have set their hearts on this principle, we never would have known the horrors that plague this world.

We rob ourselves of a correct posture with God because our attitudes sour as a result of our fleshly outlook on our lives. We say we have faith, yet worry about money, relationships, and daily struggles as if God is absent. These are not just problems, they are indicators of a misplaced focus. If we are going to be a people of substance, we must shift our attitudes and behaviors toward God and His word. Because if we don't, all that we sing and play about is a lie because we don't believe. The music ministry must be evidence of our faith as anyone should see God active in our lives.

So, in letting God arise, notice your worst enemy lives within. With that, Satan's tactic of lies and diversion is the same playbook he used on his followers in heaven. A foundation built on the Rock is what will guarantee success. Spiritually, slumber and the absence of sobriety are much more than pretexts as it does not take much to be lost. If His ways are not our ways and His thoughts not ours, we should be subject to what God has given us for our success in Him.

Life Trajectory

God has granted each person a unique life trajectory, a framework of principles that shapes and governs their existence. These principles are rooted in divine law, and our lives are meant to align with God's creative order, unfolding according to His will and pleasure. We are not all created with the same strengths or circumstances, and our differences reflect the diversity of God's design. A curse is vain and backward and a blessing is productive and forward. Adopting another person's guiding principles, without discernment, may result in confusion or even self-inflicted setbacks, as what suits one individual may not be suitable for another.

Truth is universal, whereas opinions are subjective and personal. Within this divinely ordained framework, what constitutes sin for one person may not necessarily be the same for another, depending on the specific principles God has assigned to them. Each person is called to live according to their own divine guidance, and we are responsible for honoring our unique path while allowing others the freedom to do the same. You may observe someone else's actions and deem them inconsistent with Scripture. Yet, even when motivated by good intentions, our attempts to correct others may cause more harm than good. We do not always understand another person's divine purpose, nor are we often equipped with the insight or foresight required to guide them. Never assume any authority as all authority is given by God. Many have become disillusioned with the church because mankind has, at times, weaponized it as a tool for control and domination. This distortion of purpose reflects an attempt to usurp God's rightful position as Lord. This is the spirit of the anti-Christ. Creation continues to elevate themselves above divine governance. In this, we have forgotten the truth of *Ezekiel 18:4*.

God has designed us for prosperity, and all who are in the music ministry should be prosperous. True prosperity is found within the will of God, which is inherently woven into our life's trajectory. When we encounter things we do not understand, it is wisdom, not weakness, to leave such matters in God's hands. God always has a certain way of dealing with things. Understanding will come in due time, if it is meant for us. While we may be inclined to evaluate others, our primary focus should remain on our own walk with God. God's music ministry is holy and you can find that God has a significant record of turning individuals out the way or killing people who mishandle holy things. If we become distracted or disconnected from God's will, we risk mismanaging this sacred calling. Reverence, humility, and attentiveness are essential to honoring the holiness of the music ministry entrusted to us.

Words

In Michael Jackson's song *Billie Jean*, there's a line that puzzled me for a long time. We often speak about the power of words, yet collectively, we remain unaware of just how true that is. A lie can only exist because truth exists first. Truth stands on its own, anchored in reality, and it is precisely this foundation that ensures a lie, however enduring it may seem, cannot withstand the test of time.

Every word and action is ultimately accountable to truth. This is balance, and is why we see *Deuteronomy 32:4*. Truth governs the cosmos, it is the standard by which all things are measured. Hence all reason we are called to walk in the light. Fraudulence has a shelf life. Eventually, the performer becomes the performance. What we declare, whether in truth or falsehood, shapes who we become.

I've watched people morph into the very thing they accused others of being. I'm generally uninterested in hearing what people say about others, unless it's edifying. Still, I don't immediately dismiss accusations or gossip. Why? Because in many cases, people aren't truly speaking about someone else, they're revealing themselves. Gossip and slander are often confessions in disguise. They point more to the weakness of the speaker than the character of the subject. This is how I assess those around me, and govern my response accordingly.

One of the clearest signs of immaturity and weakness, natural or spiritual, is the tendency to attack or belittle one's spouse. Words are spiritual instruments, they create, destroy, and bind. The word of God repeatedly underscores their power. When criticism becomes habitual, it carves a destructive path in a relationship. What many think is an objective commentary on their partner's shortcomings is, more often than not, a mirror held up to their own internal condition. The heart always speaks eventually, and what lives in the heart will manifest in life.

He said, "...be careful what you do, cause the lie becomes the truth..." I struggled to reconcile the idea of a lie becoming truth, until I witnessed individuals making accusations against others, only to gradually become the very thing they had condemned. It didn't happen overnight. It was a slow, almost imperceptible transformation, but it was real. This reveals our lack of caution and discernment, particularly in light of the teaching found in *Matthew 13:37-38*.

I was repeatedly criticized for the way I maintained my car, and this went on for months. At the time, I was fresh out of high school, just beginning to navigate adulthood and learn important responsibilities. Eventually, I grew tired of the constant remarks and told them to stop. Ironically, years later, they struggled to take care of their own car, while I was the one who maintained the cleaner and more well-kept vehicle.

Former friends of my wife mistreated her due to her economic circumstances at the time. They were thriving and had an optimistic outlook on life. Years later, after my wife had become highly successful, she happened to encounter them again, only to find that their social and financial situations had significantly declined.

We should exercise greater caution when "telling it like it is," as we may not understand the situation as clearly as we believe. Grasping the truth is often a gradual process rather than an immediate realization.

Music, by its very nature, is relational. And in the realm of ministry, its power lies not just in sound but in spirit. For a music ministry to be truly effective, powerful, transformative, it must be rooted in purpose and spiritual discernment. What we say, how we act, and especially how we respond in emotionally charged moments, either honors God or grieves Him. In the end, our words do not only echo, they shape lives. Be careful with what you say. Your words make you.

Attitude

Pastor Charles Swindoll once said, *"Life is 10% what happens to you and 90% how you react."* Death is inevitable, there's no escaping it, but your response to life's challenges is entirely within your control. You can view trials as endings, or you can allow them to awaken something deeper within you. Perspective is power. The way you interpret life shapes the way you live it. That's why if you truly want to pursue your dreams, you must begin with belief, establish clear goals, and commit to a timeline. Vision without structure is wishful thinking.

Scripture tells us we are God's children, so why do so many of His children fail to experience the success He designed for them? The answer often lies in misplaced identity. Too many believers walk in doubt, not faith, unaware of who they really are. The Word of God is meant to govern both lives and systems, but the reality is sobering: the ratio of *ain'ts* to *saints* remains far too high.

Psalm 100 is a powerful anchor for music ministry. No matter what chaos swirls around us, God could have placed us in entirely different circumstances. We didn't choose Him, He chose us. And if He chose us, we should respond with hearts full of gratitude. Ministry begins with surrender, and it becomes truly effective when we step outside ourselves and commit all that we are to His service.

God often places us in uncomfortable circumstances not to punish us, but to grow us, strategically shaping us for His purpose. When we understand that we are His workmanship, we can trust that everything we face is part of His divine plan. Our role is simple: trust, obey, and cultivate a posture of gratitude. Music ministry demands joy. Given the significance of our ministry, we should work to maintain a bright, warm, and welcoming spirit. Life may wear us down, but people depend on us for our smiles and comfort. A part of our ministry is to lighten up the atmosphere. While tears may visit us at times, frowns have no place. Let God handle the battle; it is, after all, the Lord's.

One of the greatest revelations we can receive is this: we must learn to see ourselves as God sees us. Since He created us, we already possess what's needed to fulfill His will. Still, we live in a culture steeped in negativity. Society has trained us to dread Mondays, expect dysfunction, and embrace pessimism. But every day is a gift. Every breath is evidence that God is still in control. Life isn't void of struggle, but there's far more good than we often recognize. Shift your focus, and your world begins to change. Above all, we are empowered by the Holy Spirit, through whom we can do all things.

One highly recommended book for all believers is *See You at the Top* by Zig Ziglar. It offers timeless insights that are especially valuable for those involved in the music ministry which is not suited for individuals who carry a negative mindset. Personally, I'm less concerned with whether the glass is half full or half empty. What matters to me is that the glass serves its purpose. If it doesn't, alternatives are available. Musicians must carry not just skill, but conviction in order for their service to be spiritually effective. The enemy specializes in psychological warfare, and many believers have fallen prey to his tactics. But through Christ, *the way, the truth, and the life,* we are more than conquerors.

Your testimony and your purpose are the driving forces behind your ministry. When you sing or play, you are ministering from the sum total of your life, the trials you've endured, the victories you've claimed, the faith that sustains you. Give everything in every moment. Worship isn't about presentation, it's surrender. Living an honest life means serving God from the heart and allowing Him to cleanse us as we worship. Let us remember that we are all human, and humanity is marked by both great potential and significant flaws. We work together, embracing these imperfections.

Borderline Personality Disorder is just one of several mental disorders that can lead individuals to inflict harm on themselves. Lupus and Multiple Sclerosis are two of various diseases that cause the body to attack itself. Are we not the body of Christ?

Forgiveness

Another book that I recommend is *The Science of Revenge: Understanding the World's Deadliest Addiction-and How to Overcome It* by James Kimmel Jr. Sanctification is a continuous process, and there is no salvation without genuine repentance, which is an act of the heart. While repentance is the essential first step in salvation, it is important to recognize that living for God is a lifelong journey marked by continual growth and transformation as we come to better understand and know God and ourselves. True repentance is the decision from the heart to change direction —leaving the past behind and moving forward. We all have stumbled in and out of church but because of God's mercy toward us, we must be able to extend grace to others.

Seventy times seven. As imperfect beings, we fall repeatedly, and if a musician cannot forgive, they will lose their ministry; as it is written, "...and, forgive us our debts as we forgive our debtors." The parable of the unmerciful servant offers perspective on how God views our forgiveness of one another. If we genuinely desire to be like Christ, we forgive because we have been pardoned ourselves. Too often, we fail to forgive those who act toward us in ways similar to how we have acted toward others.

Evaluate *Psalm 103:12* as this verse highlights the depth of God's forgiveness. Forgiveness does not necessarily mean forgetting the offense, but rather that the memory of the wrongdoing no longer holds power over us. True forgiveness enables emotional, mental, and spiritual freedom, allowing one to avoid revisiting or reliving the pain of past experiences. These experiences often shape our behavior and lead us to act with greater wisdom and caution. For those who have been saved, if they sin, sincere repentance and a deliberate turning away from that sin allows the redemptive power of Christ's blood to provide covering and restoration.

It takes effort to throw stones, yet we too often find ourselves dedicating so much time and energy to it, despite having our own lives to tend to. We are all born in sin, and the church is designed to serve the sick and disabled, a spiritual hospital. Humanity cannot escape its nature. We are not all the same, and each of us has the right to our own thoughts, with pastors given to us by God according to His heart. We are all created differently, according to God's design and what pleases Him. If you are dissatisfied with God's creation, you are in the wrong universe, and that has been tested. God brings us together and expects us to be responsible, working in love and respect for one another, knowing that we each have unique contributions to make in His work. True love for the work of God will not seek its destruction. However, discernment must be rooted in self-awareness. Sometimes we suspect others of having hidden motives not because they do—but because our own hearts are conflicted. Not every disagreement is demonic. Not every challenge is an attack. While there are certainly agents of the enemy, simply feeling challenged by a teammate does not mean they are working with the enemy. We should all be familiar with *Proverbs 18:21*, especially those in the music ministry.

If a member of your church committed adultery and had someone murdered, would you be proud to say they are part of your congregation? If someone responsible for harassing, disrupting, and persecuting your church came to your home claiming that God had sent them to seek your help, would you accept them? Could you welcome someone who tried to harm you or a loved one if God chose them to assist you in some way? Could you accept a former adulterer, violent street criminal, and inmate as your pastor?

We often judge by appearance, forgetting that God doesn't use our standards. His choices often disrupt our expectations. Is it possible that someone with tattoos and earrings may want to know Christ? If their hairstyle offends you, do you believe God does not want them? Can you accept that God does many things you may not believe He does and that He orchestrates what many cannot accept? God does not recognize our criteria. Who are we to determine what is and is not of God? Could you accept the people God chooses to bring into your life, regardless of their background? Are you strong enough to challenge your own assumptions about what God is doing? Regardless of what the situation, never assume someone's fate. We cannot foresee how God may choose to work in someone's life, and if we are not mindful, we may end up mistreating someone who is ultimately called to become one of God's most significant instruments.

It is also essential that we view ourselves through the lens of truth. None of us are perfect; according to the bible, all of us have transgressed in some way. When we come to truly recognize our flaws, we must possess the humility to acknowledge them and seek repentance. Pride presents a significant obstacle in this process. It has led many to persist in error rather than admit wrongdoing. While acknowledging fault and repenting should be seen as painless acts, pride often inflates these actions into something far more difficult to do than they need to be. At its core, pride is often a defense mechanism an effort to maintain a façade and avoid vulnerability. Ironically, this only deepens our sense of inadequacy. Frequently, our unwillingness to confront the truth stems from a lack of self-worth, which is itself often rooted in unresolved experiences from our past. If we want God's help, we must face the truth.

Therefore, we also must extend grace to ourselves. All of us have a past, and we are all dealing with trauma on some level, and many who are singing and playing in the music ministry have not reconciled with past situations and the person they used to be. Being a new creature means we are no longer who we once were. How can we fully let it go for others if we have not done so for ourselves? We were who we were at that time for whatever reason and God, through His mercy, delivered us. We cannot continue to cling to our past if we are to move forward. To truly minister and be free in music, we must not allow anything to hold us back or keep us in bondage. We will always struggle with the flesh; God assures us that His grace is sufficient. As leaders, we must push through and press forward.

Sammy Davis Jr. delivers a powerful message in his song that all believers should pay attention to: you are uniquely who you are, even if you stand alone, and you can be no one else. God takes great pleasure in the way He created each of us. Therefore, we must learn to accept ourselves as we are. God chooses whom He wills and removes those who are disobedient, yet no one else can fulfill your purpose as effectively as you can, because it is uniquely yours.

Leaders

Leaders are people managers and they set the environment for the participants. When issues arise, the leader must first examine themselves and identify where they may have missed it, as the leader shoulders the blame. The spirit of the leader influences the entire group. Therefore, it is essential for leaders to have a clear vision and the ability to communicate it effectively, creating a stable environment that allows team members to thrive. Accountability is key. When things go awry, the leader must maintain integrity, demonstrate compassion, seek understanding, and work collaboratively with those involved without showing partiality, toward a peaceful resolution.

Ministers must be at the forefront, and to qualify for leadership positions, they must be deeply engaged in the church's business and ministries. This includes regularly volunteering, assisting with ongoing activities, and consistently offering support, whether monetary, physical, or spiritual. They are the most significant servants, the lowest person in the highest position with a spirit of service and strong spiritual qualities.

To lead in God's work is a sacred privilege, not a platform for control. Leadership in the Kingdom does not permit mistreatment or disregard for others. Every individual under your care deserves respect. A true leader honors those they lead, taking the time to listen, learn, and uplift. Leadership, at its core, is service wrapped in humility and powered by love.

CHAPTER FOUR

SEX

But fornication, and all uncleanness, or covetousness, let it not be once named among you as becometh saints. Neither filthiness, or foolish talking, nor jesting, which are not convenient: but rather giving of thanks. For this ye know, that no whoremonger, nor unclean person, nor covetous man, who is an idolater, hath any inheritance in the kingdom of Christ and of God.

Ephesians 5:3-5 KJV

For this cause God gave them up to vile affections: for even their women did change the natural use into that which is against nature: and likewise also the men, leaving the natural use of the woman, burned in their lust one toward another; men with men working that which is unseemly, and receiving in themselves that recompense of their error which was meet. And even as they did not like to retain God in their knowledge, God gave them over to a reprobate mind to do those things which are not convenient;

Romans 1:26-28 KJV

But from the beginning of the creation God made them male and female. For this cause shall a man leave his father and mother, and cleave to his wife; and they twain shall be one flesh: so then they are no more twain, but one flesh. What therefore God hath joined together, let not man put asunder.
Mark 10:6-9 KJV

And they were both naked, the man and his wife, and were not ashamed.
Genesis 2:25 KJV

Be not deceived; God is not mocked: for whatsoever a man soweth, that shall he also reap. For he that soweth to his flesh shall of the flesh reap corruption; but he that soweth to the Spirit shall of the Spirit reap life everlasting. And let us not be weary in well doing: for in due season we shall reap, if we faint not. As we have therefore opportunity, let us do good unto all men, especially unto them who are of the household of faith.
Galatians 6:7-10 KJV

Hell

Jesus Christ, the Son of God, unequivocally affirmed the reality of a literal place called hell, a place of intense, unrelenting torment reserved for those who reject the truth of God's Word. Many tribulations in this life cause people to question the existence of God. However, disobedience comes with a heavy and painful price. Always reflect on *Galatians 6:7-8*, as many have destroyed their lives through foolishness and ignorance. All decisions carry either reward or consequences. No one has the right or the ability to dismiss a principle. If understanding is needed, seek it from the one who possesses all wisdom, and accept the answer as He gives it.

Many fail to grasp the significance of *Ecclesiastes 8:11* and *Romans 6:23*. Sin is a nature embedded in the heart of humanity, leading to actions known as sins. An act of obedience or disobedience generates a spiritual event that unfolds over time. Each act of sin is missing the mark in one way or another. Consequences of an act of sin can play out years later and it will affect others. What we do literally changes our nature. Too many in the music department ministering with the wrong nature because of what they practice.

God enters the human heart through His Word and by divine process, His Word cleanses the heart. The heart is inherently depraved and unclean, while God is perfectly holy. He does not override human free will; rather, He calls individuals to take responsibility for their own hearts. *Psalm 119:11* reminds us of this. Through His Word, He reveals Himself as Lord and Savior. So what, then, is His Word?

If God had made room for sin, there would be no need for Jesus Christ. The Almighty God is the supreme governance and creative power of, and in the universe, and His son was given in death as a substitute for humanity. The Holy Ghost overshadowed Mary. The Holy Ghost is the spirit of God, not another entity. Jesus had to be without sin, and sin is passed down through a man, not a woman, which is why the Holy Ghost had to be the father-all detailed in *Matthew*. The spirit in Jesus, the man who was made a little lower than the angles, was God Himself, hence Emmanuel. That is how Jesus knew the conversation between two dead men and was able to perform miracles.

If Jesus had become sin, he would not have qualified to be our sacrifice. *2 Corinthians 5:21* and *Isaiah 53:6* tells us Jesus was made the sin offering. All his blood was given on the cross for an atonement for the soul. This is the New Testament where we may receive remission of sins through the essential practice of baptism in the Lord Jesus Christ's name. Innocence was the price for reconciliation. Jesus gave up the spirit in him and was resurrected when the spirit of God reentered that body, and He walked on earth in a spiritual body three days later with wounds that shed no blood. This is how Jesus Christ is the first born from the dead and is Lord of all now.

The issue of free will must be carefully considered, as individuals we have the ability to make their own choices. However, while one may choose freely, the consequences of those choices often lie beyond personal control. As free moral agents, we are responsible for our decisions, but fulfilling one's purpose and living a life devoted to God requires obedience. True success is not defined by freedom alone, but by submission to divine instruction. Ultimately, we each have the freedom to decide whether we will live in such a way to merit the words, "Well done, thou good and faithful servant."

The most formidable adversary in your life is not the devil, demons, or even other people. It's you. You will make decisions that will determine your destiny. It's easier to blame and turn away from others than it is to turn on yourself. No cross, no life. *Matthew 25:41* and *Revelation 20* should impress upon anyone the reality of everlasting punishment with fire. We all have our lives before God and we must be careful of the decisions we make and consider a question impressed upon me time and again from my pastor, the late Bishop Jeremiah Reed, *"Where will YOU be when YOU get where YOU'RE goin'?"*

Take careful notice when I talk about your life trajectory. With this comes your life autobiography which the angel in heaven is keeping your account in your book written in heaven. Everyone will be required to give an account of their lives. It's crucial to remember that we will be judged not only by our actions, but also by our intentions and the outcomes they produce. Reference *Ecclesiastes 12:13-14*.

Wrongful sexual acts in the music ministry have tied down many and have caused serious issues in churches and in their lives. These actions have fostered confusion and led many to lose faith in the church. God will hold everyone accountable, as every word and deed is recorded in our life book, which will be sealed and presented for judgment at the end of our lives. The church is not a place for dating games or casual experiments in seeking boyfriends or girlfriends for the sake of fun or pleasure. Your outlook should be, God will provide the right one for me in His time. *Jeremiah 17:9-10* is a death sentence for many in the music ministry.

Nakedness

Whoever God places in a leadership position their spirit will set the tone for governance. Adam was given dominion over the world and there was no shame of sin because humanity's relationship with God was perfect; there was nothing to hide. But he lost that relationship with God when he failed to keep the word of the Lord. As a result, death entered the world, cursing the earth and condemning the natural body. Due to this spiritual transgression, humanity bears the natural shame of sin. Nakedness now represents the loss of spiritual power, and in the natural world, we must be clothed. While the Holy Ghost provides us with spiritual clothing, the natural body remains unredeemed and continues to decay. To publicly expose one's natural nakedness is to reveal both sacredness and shame. Sharing this nakedness with the same sex, including self-pleasure, serves to debase and defile oneself. In honor and reverence for what is holy, natural nakedness is reserved solely for your spouse of the opposite sex. This is not just a matter of morals or personal opinions, but of adhering to God's principles.

Music in the church is not intended for entertainment or self-expression, nor is it an art form. It's meant for worship. The experience of music is an awesome phenomenon and is designed to be. But that high is not to be perverted. Sexual attraction is a natural aspect of humanity. While sex is undeniably a pleasurable experience, it serves a purpose: the procreation of humanity. This purpose is explicitly stated in *Genesis*, where it commands us to "be fruitful and multiply," which also means that sexual relations with inanimate objects are unrighteous.

Many of us view marriage through the lens of sex, without fully considering God's reasoning for marriage. While fleeing fornication is a valid reason, marriage is ultimately meant to help us fulfill our greater purpose. God has endowed us with gifts and abilities for His work, yet there are certain aspects of this purpose that may not be fully realized by someone living a single life. God created Adam and Eve to be companions who would support and fulfill each other's purpose—Adam's purpose, which in turn became Eve's as well. As we seek a mate, we must trust that God has already designated someone who will help us carry out our purpose on earth.

Nakedness, physical, emotional, and spiritual, is sacred, and it must remain within the boundaries God has established. The human body is a masterpiece of divine design, but sin has distorted our perception of it. Desire has been corrupted by carnality. God is calling His children to rise above the instinctual pull of the flesh, to renew their minds, and to discipline their bodies. All of this is possible through the power of the Holy Ghost.

Pornography

Your Brain on Porn: Internet Pornography and the Emerging Science of Addiction by Gary Wilson is a must-read for anyone seeking to understand the powerful intersection between neuroscience, behavior, and morality. Knowledge is leverage and when confronting deep-rooted challenges like addiction, ignorance is not an option. You can't fight with ignorance.

Pornography distorts the brain's natural chemical balance, gradually reshaping neural pathways and reinforcing destructive behavioral cycles. Repeated exposure can lead to addiction, numbing emotional sensitivity, and altering perceptions of intimacy. Those who expose their bodies for the gratification of others, just as those who consume such content, participate in a cycle of mutual degradation. In both cases, the vessel, intended for divine purpose, is dishonored and perverted.

Another profound danger lies in the quiet erosion of desire for genuine intimacy. With prolonged exposure to pornography, the brain's natural chemistry begins to shift, gradually rewiring sexual appetite toward artificial and often distorted fantasies. What begins as visual stimulation can quickly evolve into a reliance on illusion, where the imagination, flooded with scripted, exaggerated scenarios, replaces the need for real connection. Over time, this dependency can hollow out authentic sexual experiences, leaving behind a counterfeit version of intimacy that no longer satisfies the heart, mind, or soul. Imagination is the residence of lust.

Scientific research now supports what many spiritual beliefs have long held: habitual pornography use can erode empathy, distort emotional connections, and reduce the human person to an object. As users become more conditioned to artificial and often aggressive portrayals of sex, they grow detached from the relational and sacred dimensions of human connection and love. Over time, these effects may contribute to anxiety, depression, and in severe cases, suicidal ideation. The mind becomes haunted by distorted ideals, while the soul wrestles with an internal misalignment from its original design.

From a theological perspective, this is not simply a psychological or social dilemma, it's a spiritual crisis. The body is a sacred vessel, created to honor the Creator, not to be misused or objectified for fleeting pleasure. Pornography undermines that purpose, encouraging the violation of personal boundaries, the exploitation of others, and the devaluation of conventional love. It is, in every sense, a war against the sacred.

Modern digital culture has made sexually explicit content pervasive. Not only are individuals exposed to graphic imagery with increasing frequency, but public and online spaces now often normalize behaviors that were once considered taboo. Group sex, orgies, voyeurism, real life explicit content, across both heterosexual and LGBTQ expressions, are now accessible to audiences of all ages, including the impressionable minds of youth.

This raises a sobering question: What are we teaching the next generation about sex, love, and identity? The shaping of young minds ultimately shapes the future of culture and principle. When children and teens are introduced to sexuality through pornography, they risk internalizing a world view that divorces physical intimacy from emotional connection, responsibility, and love.

Love is not lust. Love, in its truest form, is commitment, rooted in truth, grounded in selflessness, and anchored in purpose, a principle of affection deep in the heart. It is this divine model of love that pornography seeks to corrupt. Many believe that the distortion of sexuality is one of the enemy's most effective tools, a means of turning the sacred into spectacle, and the meaningful into mere gratification.

As a society and as individuals, we must reclaim the sacredness of the body, the beauty of conventional love, and the power of purity, not out of shame or repression, but out of reverence for what was divinely intended.

Sex

Pornography is not the sole catalyst for sexual immorality; rather, such behavior ultimately stems from the deeper issue of the human heart. It reflects desires that extend beyond the boundaries of what many believe God has designed for human sexuality. In extreme cases, these distorted desires may even involve children, revealing the extent of moral decay in society. Many look out into the world and say, "These are the last days," and lament that the world is coming to an end. Interestingly, all the signs of "the end" can also be found within the church. God has given every individual a conscience, a moral compass intended to serve as a safeguard. However, when individuals repeatedly ignore or override their conscience, it can become dulled or even silenced, leading them to engage in behaviors they might once have found unthinkable. *2 Timothy 3* is dealing with those in the church, saints.

Sex is intended to be a sacred act, a profound physical expression of love within a meaningful and committed relationship. However, in modern society, this sacredness has often been perverted, distorted, and commercialized, leading to significant consequences for individuals and communities. Within the music and entertainment industries, sexual expression is frequently portrayed as a form of art, empowerment, or self-expression, yet this portrayal can have powerful and often negative influences and have caused many to be subject to spirits that have them trapped and doomed for destruction. While some seek freedom through counseling or therapy, these methods fall short when addressing spiritual issues. We are vessels, created not only with physical and emotional dimensions but also with spiritual dimensions. Thus, we are susceptible to spiritual influence. The only power that can help is the power of the Lord Jesus Christ. As articulated in the book of *Isaiah*, the anointing destroys the yoke.

Fornication is all illegal sexual acts and adultery is a spouse engaging in an illegal sexual act. Marriage is intended to be a sacred and pure union, both physically and spiritually. When that sanctity is compromised, the relationship becomes adulterated, no longer whole or undefiled. Marriage represents a spiritual bond, and when that connection is shared with someone other than one's spouse, it constitutes adultery, even in the absence of physical intimacy. One can live in a state of adultery through emotional or spiritual entanglements, as these connections often originate in the heart. Such ties can be deeply felt, regardless of physical proximity, and maintaining the purity of this bond is essential. Jesus Christ addresses this concept in the Gospels, emphasizing that even lustful intent in the heart is adulterous, thereby broadening the traditional understanding of fidelity.

Spiritual connections bring people together and under certain circumstances, illegal spiritual practices. This may help explain why some events or behaviors seem to "just happen" without clear rationale. You know when that "thing" hits and kind of takes you over? That is why some cannot stop masturbating. Without discernment and vigilance, individuals may find themselves influenced by negative spiritual forces, often without realizing it. This influence can lead people to engage in actions they once believed were beyond them. Individuals who are influenced by similar spiritual forces are drawn to one another, what some refer to as kindred spirits. Spirits recognize each other. These connections can foster a sense of unity and drive collective behaviors, including participation in activities such as group sexual encounters and parties and other morally questionable acts. Deliverance from these spirits is also what church is for. However, when members, particularly those in influential positions such as the music ministry compromise their spiritual integrity, the church's ability to function effectively in this role will be hindered. The job of the enemy is to steal, kill and destroy.

LGBTQ

Another "thing," is same sex engagement. God created two humans. One male and the other, one female, and established this binary as the foundation for human relationships and reproduction. Within this framework, the blessing and sacredness of sex are understood to exist within the context of a heterosexual union. In the beginning God blessed male and female. God blesses the union of male and female, setting a precedent for human intimacy and family structure. An individual's gender is not fluid but fixed, determined by the immutable genetic blueprint assigned at conception.

God clearly does not tolerate LGBTQ behavior. God has never made room for LGBTQ except for repentance. By divine design, human reproduction requires both a male's sperm and a female's egg, a principle that remains fundamental regardless of social or ideological perspectives. Masturbation is self-pleasure which is same sex pleasure and that stands in stark contrast for the purpose of a heterosexual relationship. Yet a spirit of deception has contributed to widespread confusion, leading some to question or reject these foundational truths about human identity and sexuality.

Many individuals who support the LGBTQ movement may do so out of a lack of understanding or because they find it difficult to embrace what some believe to be objective moral or spiritual truth. Some may simply be unaware of alternative perspectives grounded in religious teachings. Others just want to do it. However, responding with anger, hostility, or hatred toward the LGBTQ community will not help. Genuine, godly love, expressed through compassion, patience, and truth is essential for meaningful dialogue and transformation. Only through love can bridges be built and hearts potentially opened to different understandings.

There are people who venture into practices that leave them spiritually bound and powerless to break free despite a sincere desire to live rightly. The struggle against "spiritual wickedness in high places" is profound, there is no place higher than the church. Generations have suffered at the hands of those they trusted: authority figures, teachers, family members, and others who, driven by personal depravity, have exploited the vulnerable for their own gratification and gain. Such experiences have understandably led many victims to develop a distorted understanding of God, and in their pain, some have turned to alternative belief systems or chosen to reject faith altogether in an attempt to cope with deep trauma.

Regrettably, the very institution meant to be a refuge, the church, has been complicit in this harm. For selfish and fleshly motives, individuals within positions of spiritual influence have abused the trust of those seeking healing, connection, and salvation. Particularly concerning is the presence of such misconduct among those in the music ministry, singers, musicians, and others, whose public devotion masks private deception. They play and sing of Christ while their lifestyles reflect allegiance to another kingdom. Their actions betray the sacred trust they carry, turning a ministry of worship into a platform of spiritual compromise.

Indecency

Judgment is proportional to the act although the outcome of what you do is always much greater. This is the process of sin. The single act of disobedience from Adam cost the world. Death is separation from life and God is life. As a result, being born naturally gets you here but another birth of the spirit is what reconnects you to God. The curse is that God turned man to his own mind, a mind disconnected from infinite thought and power. Now humanity is enslaved to its own desires. The Old Testament is not simply a collection of historical texts. The Old Testament is the covenant between God's people, the *Hebrews*, for salvation. The New Testament replaced the old covenant because of Jesus Christ. His word and His laws are eternal and all who violate His laws and those who transgress them are subject to divine judgment.

Human behavior is shaped by what resides within us. The Kingdom of God refers to the governance of God's laws operating internally, from the heart. When this inner rule is aligned with one's conscience, it fosters harmony with God. However, many individuals believe they have been saved, yet struggle to overcome the desires of the flesh. This struggle often stems from a lack of spiritual power, which is imparted through the Holy Ghost. Without genuine repentance, individuals remain accountable for their past sins, even if they have been baptized in the name of Jesus Christ. In such cases, remission of sins has not occurred.

This is a day of corruption where sexual taste is extravagant, and barriers are no more. The prevailing cultural mindset increasingly treats sex as a casual act, divorced from its moral and spiritual implications. God's laws are His creative authority and are designed to guide humanity toward flourishing and order. When individuals deviate from these divine principles, the result is not only moral decline but also spiritual degradation. Such choices can lead to inner turmoil, a corrupted nature, and vulnerability to destructive influences that distort perception and behavior. This concept is strongly reinforced in biblical texts such as *Leviticus 18*, which outlines explicit boundaries concerning sexual conduct. Engaging in acts such as incest or bestiality, leads to a profoundly disordered nature and spirit. We all are born with a fallen nature, and every action carries spiritual consequences. Thus, behavior that contradicts divine principles ultimately results in judgment.

Pleasure naturally comes with sex but the volatility of sin and the extent of lust have driven saints to practices that have greatly vexed God. It's unnatural, and a grave violation of principle for anyone to seek sexual gratification with an animal, as human sexuality was designed for union between humans, particularly within the context of procreation and covenant. Animals are meant to reproduce within their own kind, and any deviation from this order is a violation of divine intention. Some individuals, driven by misguided desire, seek pleasure through inanimate objects such as pillows, stuffed animals, mattresses, or other items that lack any meaningful connection to human intimacy or purpose. Such behaviors are seen as expressions of a deeper spiritual disorder. When a person is overtaken by malicious spiritual influences, pleasure becomes disconnected from principle and their desires become misdirected, often leading them to make dangerous and degrading choices.

All individuals are born with innate tendencies, and what attracts one person may not attract another. Genetically and temperamentally, certain traits or types of people naturally draw our attention, and our sources of excitement or interest can vary widely. Fetishes, specific personal preferences or sources of sexual pleasure, are highly individualized and, from a biblical perspective, are intended to be explored exclusively within the context of marriage between a man and a woman. In today's highly stimulating environment, it's easy to become distracted by what we see and experience. Without a strong foundation in God's word and spiritual discipline, individuals may lack the inner strength required to resist temptation. In the absence of this foundation, people are more likely to make poor decisions, potentially leading to morally and spiritually destructive outcomes.

It's widely acknowledged that both men and women, through various means and degrees of access, have sexually exploited children. In some cases, even family members have enabled or ignored these abuses within their own circles. Such actions inflict deep and lasting trauma, often resulting in the severe disruption of a child's psychological and emotional development. Children must never be subjected to sexual contact, nor should they be encouraged to explore or express alternate gender identities in ways that undermine their innocence and developmental integrity. Children hold a sacred place in the heart of God. Scripture teaches that vengeance belongs to God, underscoring the gravity of harming the innocent. Children not only represent the future of humanity, they are the future of humanity. Tragically, many adults continue to carry the wounds of childhood abuse, striving to move forward in life while still wrestling with the deep pain and consequences of their past lives and experiences.

Victims of abuse should first understand that God sees their pain and, despite how unjust the experience may be, He can bring purpose and healing from even the most devastating situations. There is a sovereign God, and in time, all things will be made right. Second, it is crucial for survivors to know that what happened to them is not their fault. They should hold their heads high and allow God to redeem their story, using their experiences to support and encourage others who have faced similar trauma. The fact that such suffering occurred does not mean they were rejected by God. On the contrary, God's nature is the highest good, and His love remains constant. Redemption is a process.

Emotions, while deeply human, are not the same as principles. Principles are rooted in divine laws, while feelings fluctuate with circumstances. Seeking counseling or therapy is a responsible and constructive step toward healing from trauma, and it should be encouraged within both faith-based and broader communities. Suicide is never the answer. Each life is divinely created and carries purpose. Even when life feels overwhelming, God remains present, orchestrating all things according to His will. He has not abandoned those who suffer. While God allows human beings the freedom to make their own choices, sometimes resulting in harm, He is also a just God, and in due time, He will bring justice and deliverance. Suffering hardship is the process of buying success.

If you are in crisis or need immediate help, call 988, the Suicide & Crisis Lifeline. God, in His love and wisdom, has made resources available to provide a way of escape and support. God is love. If you are feeling unloved or abandoned, turn to prayer. God always hears, and He will respond, though often in His timing, not ours. When that response comes, it will be at the perfect moment, even if it's not immediately clear. It's important to confront and work through feelings of anger or disappointment toward God. Holding on to that anger can deepen emotional pain and prolong healing. Trusting in God's plan requires faith, especially when circumstances are difficult. If God had truly rejected you, you would not be alive. Your very existence is evidence that He still has a purpose for you. Though the path may be painful, healing and restoration are possible, and in time, it will work out for your good.

At the same time, other critical issues must be addressed, as the prevailing spirit of this age has deeply affected the moral and psychological fabric of society. Voluntary incest, while often overlooked, has become alarmingly pervasive, and it's a destructive and harmful practice. In some cases, individuals who identify as homosexual or lesbian have been shaped by early sexual experiences involving inappropriate relationships between parents and children, such as fathers and sons or mothers and daughters and other family members. These are not just moral failures, they are soul wounds. Such trauma must be named, confronted, and healed.

There are troubling instances where younger individuals have initiated or responded to sexual advances from their parents, and vice versa. In some cases, adult sons and daughters have solicited their parents, and siblings, both young and old, have engaged in sexual behavior with one another. Numerous cases also involve other family members willingly participating in illicit sexual conduct. These behaviors raise serious moral and psychological concerns, and it's especially disturbing that some individuals express satisfaction or pleasure in such deviant acts. Addressing these matters requires both moral clarity and compassionate support for healing and restoration.

The practice of married couples engaging in partner-swapping, commonly referred to as swinging, has become increasingly normalized in certain social circles. However, such behavior is incompatible with the values expected of those who identify as children of the Most High. Participating in activities such as vacations to clothing-optional resorts, nude cruises, or similar events reflects a focus on carnal desires rather than spiritual discipline. Publicly displaying one's nakedness not only undermines personal dignity but also brings dishonor to the church. According to the epistles, our bodies do not belong to us; all souls belong to God, and believers are reminded that they have been bought with a price.

People explore non-monogamous relationships but when God made man, he gave him one woman. Now we are where humanity has populated the earth as God has designed and God is requiring a monogamist relationship. Polygamous relationships are not what God designed. God set the requirements for a king over His people to only have one wife. We can come up with many reasons to do what we want to do but no argument can override the permanence of His word in *Psalms 119:89.*

Modesty matters. Worship is a sacred space where distractions must be minimized. Revealing clothing, tight attire that exposes genital outlines, or garments that sexualize the body, especially in ministry, are incompatible with reverence. The pulpit is not a place for entertainment. There is an appropriate time and place for everything, and it's difficult to worship sincerely under distractions such as overtly revealing clothing. Camel toe is not appropriate especially in ministry on the pulpit. Additionally, garments that expose the buttocks, often referred to colloquially as "butt floss," can be highly distracting in a worship setting. Leaving dirty underwear or engaging and similar careless behaviors in public aligns more closely with worldly indecency than with the dignity expected of God's children. Public decency should reflect spiritual dignity. We reflect what we worship.

It is important to distinguish between beauty and sexuality; they are not synonymous. Increasingly, displays meant to be "sexy" often verge on being distasteful. Any woman can attract attention through exposure, but men and women of faith are called to uphold a different standard. To conform to worldly fashions is to imitate a culture opposed to Christ. We cannot represent Christ effectively if our appearance and behavior reflect the values of the world we have been called to leave behind. Instead, God calls us to be a source of hope and light to those around us.

For the ministry of music to be truly effective, we must make decisions that allow God to have complete control. We cannot live on the edge of compromise and still expect God's blessing. While we may conceal certain behaviors from others, nothing is hidden from God. Too many people with the wrong heart and spirit come to church to explore sin and wickedness.

Who can render a good explanation to live precariously in God's service?

The Pastor

God despises vanity, and in this present age, there is no divine mandate nor legitimate reason for the continued offices of apostles or prophets. The foundation of the Church has already been laid, and the office God is actively using today is that of the pastor. The pastor is not a figure of charisma or spectacle but a divinely appointed shepherd whose role is to nurture and oversee the spiritual development of God's people.

A pastor's responsibility is to *feed* and *guide* the flock, to provide spiritual insight and care that equips believers to thrive in the Kingdom of God. This oversight is not just to be understood as administrative, it's deeply spiritual, granting the pastor discernment to identify what each soul needs in order to grow, heal, and fulfill divine purpose.

When a person receives salvation, they are not left to wander. **God assigns them a pastor,** a spiritual authority charged with their ongoing development. Rebuke and correction are not signs of rejection but rather the evidence of divine love and commitment. As Scripture teaches, "Whom the Lord loves, He chastens." To reject correction is to reject the opportunity for repentance, and without repentance, there is no salvation.

Through salvation, we are united with God, but sin causes a disconnection from Him. When this separation occurs, repentance must precede a process of restoration. *Galatians 6:1* provides guidance for this restoration, emphasizing that repentance is a necessary prerequisite to confession; without it, confession is merely a report. Since God knows and sees all, there is no need to reveal truths to Him. Confession is not about self-degradation or exposing oneself to ridicule. Rather, it involves subduing the flesh, relinquishing pride, and coming clean before the one responsible for your spiritual well-being. Enduring temporary embarrassment is insignificant compared to the gravity of facing eternal condemnation. Once you have confessed your wrong-doing to a spiritual authority, the process of restoring your relationship with God can begin. As *Proverbs* teaches, this is how you prosper.

Though pastors are human, they hold a sacred office established by God. In the Book of *Revelation*, they are referred to as "angels," emphasizing their divine charge to guide and perfect the saints. In contrast to the apostolic and prophetic offices of earlier dispensations, the pastoral office is now the primary channel through which God delivers His Word to His people.

This truth is especially critical for those serving in the music ministry. The souls of God's people are precious, purchased at a price, and entrusted to faithful stewardship. The music department is not exempt from this divine order. It must operate under pastoral authority, aligned with biblical instruction, and driven by spiritual discipline, not self-expression or entertainment. For the music ministry to flourish, it must submit to the spiritual structure God has ordained, beginning with the pastor.

The Right One

Marrying the wrong person can completely derail your life's trajectory. As a society, we have yet to fully comprehend the dangers of mismatched unions. Despite the abundance of dating apps and matchmaking platforms designed to help us find "the one," many people remain unaware of their own purpose, let alone the qualities a life partner must embody to support that purpose.

Yes, there are circumstances where divorce becomes a reality. Life is not always neat, and I speak from personal experience as I am the product of a marriage that ended in divorce. And yet, through that pain, God revealed purpose. That chapter, too, was woven into the fabric of His plan. All things work together ...

Consider the profound case study of Abraham, Sarah, and Hagar. God had promised Abraham and Sarah a son, but human logic led Sarah to offer Hagar as a surrogate, resulting in the birth of Ishmael. True faith would have waited on God, even when the promise seemed impossible. What God says will come to pass, because He cannot lie.

That one decision introduced strife into the household and led to Hagar and Ishmael's exile. Even more striking, the ripple effects of that moment echo through generations, as the descendants of Isaac and Ishmael remain in conflict to this day.

Abraham was also told to leave his country and his kin, but he brought his nephew, Lot, along. After the destruction of Sodom and Gomorrah, Lot's daughters, believing they were the last of their lineage, resorted to a desperate and disturbing act, conceiving children with their father. From those acts were born nations that would become hostile to Israel for generations.

Obedience to God is never just about one moment or one decision. It is about aligning with an eternal blueprint, one that spans time, people, and unseen outcomes. Your obedience doesn't just affect your life; it affects generations, nations, and destinies.

There are countless events and things God is orchestrating in your favor, many of which you will never see in this life. Some of them may be uncomfortable, even traumatic. But they are necessary. God could have chosen anyone, but He chose you to play a role in His divine plan. That means your pain is not pointless, it is part of the process.

Like a mother enduring the pain of childbirth to bring forth new life, pain is often the gateway to purpose. The question is not whether pain will come, but whether we trust God through it. This is when you lean into the message behind that familiar song: *"I Will Trust In The Lord."* Not just with your lips, but with your life.

Marriage

A healthy marriage is first and foremost a union of spirits. And according to divine design, spirits of the same sex cannot unite. God established the framework of marriage through Adam and Eve. It's more than a biological pairing. It is a spiritual prototype for human unity. While the journey to that union may take time, if a marriage is authored by God, its cohesion is inevitable. A God-ordained spouse will nurture the mind, body, and spirit, the complete soul, completing you in a way that fosters peace, joy, and purpose.

Today's relationship gurus offer polished quotes and popular advice, yet divorcing love from divine principle often leads to relationships marked by confusion, emotional fatigue, and unmet expectations. In God's architecture, each gender holds specific spiritual and functional roles within the marriage covenant. When both partners embrace their divine assignments, their lives form a uniquely tailored partnership, fueled not by societal molds, but by heaven's design. There is no one-size-fits-all formula. Every marriage is shaped by its own journey and the souls within it.

For a marriage to fulfill its purpose, it must be both strong and healthy. Communication is not just helpful, it is the life blood of the relationship. Likewise, sexual intimacy is not optional; it is vital. We are physical beings with emotional needs, and when those needs are consistently neglected, the door opens to discontent, emotional affairs, and eventually adultery. It is the sacred duty of each spouse to meet the other's needs with intentionality, sacrifice, and heart. You may feel frustrated or "turned off" by your spouse's behavior, but pause and ask: What am I doing (or not doing) that may be contributing to the problem?

Love is not always convenient. True love chooses to endure, to lean in, and to reconcile even when it hurts. Every meaningful union involves two flawed individuals navigating their own internal battles. Great marriages are not stumbled upon, they are built, often through hardship, patience, and forgiveness. When you genuinely love someone, you swallow the pain and figure it out.

Scripture outlines the seriousness of the marital bond and the grounds upon which divorce is permitted. A fractured marriage, especially one void of intimacy and connection, can hinder both spouses' capacity to function in ministry. Why? Because their callings are intertwined. When the relationship weakens, so does the spiritual posture necessary for serving others. Couples must therefore take ownership of their roles, practice honest dialogue, and understand that what seems unbearable in silence often becomes manageable when approached with maturity and grace. Do what is right, even when your spouse does not. Obedience always positions you for divine favor.

A thriving marriage masters two key elements: communication and intimacy, both emotional and physical. When a cell phone receives more attention than a spouse, or when partners are afraid to share their nakedness, physically or emotionally, this signals a breach that must be addressed. Ongoing neglect of sexual intimacy can lead to emotional isolation, temptation, and resentment. The Bible permits abstinence only during a woman's cycle or by mutual consent for a time of prayer. Outside of that, nothing should interfere with the physical union of husband and wife. The husband's body belongs to his wife, and the wife's body belongs to her husband. In marriage you forfeit your nakedness to your spouse.

Ministry begins at home. If a person cannot nurture their spouse, they are not fit to lead others. Your spouse is your first ministry. If your communication is more consistent with your children, friends, or even in your congregation than with your spouse, it's time to reevaluate your priorities. That which you love most receives the most communication.

If you're currently involved in music ministry, or feel called to it, now is the time to confront the hard questions. Are you whole at home? Is your marriage reflecting God's love, or hiding dysfunction behind a stage act? Healing, restoration, and effectiveness in ministry begin not with the microphone, but with the heart behind closed doors.

Human Desire

Laws within society exist to safeguard the vulnerable and promote collective well-being. For example, legal age requirements for marriage reflect more than cultural expectations, they are societal measures designed to protect individuals from exploitation and harm. The Bible speaks to the governing laws of natural government. Many of these principles should be written in our hearts, serving as an internal compass that helps preserve order, justice, and righteousness.

Governments create institutions to shield the helpless from abuse, neglect, and injustice. But above all, the Word of God stands as the supreme spiritual authority, unshakable, eternal, and divinely inspired to lead God's people in every area of life. Those called into ministry, especially those in the music ministry, must yield to these laws. No one should ever be approached inappropriately, manipulated, or violated. The church is not a stage for performance or a platform for predation, it is a sanctuary: a sacred space for healing, refuge, and restoration for the spiritually weary, wounded, and broken.

When it comes to deception, the issue isn't only spoken words, it's a matter of character. Your spirit is the real you. One cannot live a life of authentic worship while secretly harboring sin or willfully violating God's commands. Sooner or later, the truth reveals itself, often in ways that can't be hidden or controlled.

The heart is the problem as one's intentions drive actions. People deceive themselves into thinking that emotional experiences in church, singing, dancing, shouting, or speaking in tongues, automatically equate to right standing with God. But emotional elevation is not spiritual transformation. Many continue in public expressions of worship while God remains grieved and angered by the hidden life they refuse to confront.

Those who serve in music ministry, in particular, must approach their calling with sincerity, humility, and reverence. Their role is not to impress. It is essential to seek God's face earnestly, asking for a clean heart and a right spirit. God is more than able to deliver from lust, deceit, or any other bondage, but He requires truth in the inward parts.

Chapter Five

THE ANOINTING

And David said to Saul, Wherefore hearest thou men's words, saying, Behold, David seeketh thy hurt? Behold, this day thine eyes have seen how that the LORD had delivered thee to day into mine hand in the cave: and some bade me kill thee: but mine eye spared thee; and I said, I will not put forth mine hand against my lord; for he is the LORD's anointed.

1 Samuel 24:9-10 KJV

So he departed thence, and found Elisha the son of Shaphat, who was plowing with twelve yoke of oxen before him, and he with the twelfth: and Elijah passed by him, and cast his mantle upon him.

1 Kings 19:19 KJV

For the word of God is quick, and powerful, and sharper than any two edged sword, piercing even to the dividing asunder of soul and spirit, and of the joints and marrow, and is a discerner of the thoughts and intents of the heart.

Hebrews 4:12 KJV

Revelation

I have experienced moments of profound revelation, and notably, they did not occur within a church setting. Knowledge itself is not power; rather, it reflects one's relationship to information. The principle, as outlined in scripture, is that God provides pastors to feed His people with knowledge and understanding. We do not choose. Spiritual life flows from God through a divinely appointed leader and extends to all those whom God has connected to that leader. While many individuals occupy pastoral roles, not all are true pastors. People often move from church to church because they are not firmly established in the ministry where God intends them to be, leading to spiritual malnutrition and, ultimately, stagnation. As a result, many never come to the full understanding of salvation, and countless numbers of God's people are left spiritually unfulfilled or destroyed. Tragically, many of the sheep in God's flock are deprived of the care and guidance they need.

Success in the Christian walk is not akin to a short-term program, or a 12-month workout regimen followed by graduation. It is a lifelong commitment, during which you may find yourself grappling with the same challenges for extended periods. Just as children do not mature overnight, teaching and training over time produce individuals of character. To qualify for spiritual growth and maturity, one must first invest the necessary time and effort. As you mature spiritually, your appetites change. God has made a profound investment in His people and expects a return. The Word of God serves as the spiritual seed, which, over time, takes root in the heart. At the appointed time, God reveals a deeper understanding of His Word, leading to revelation. Revelation is not just new information, it is truth unveiled. This revealing of truth changes your status of holding information to perceiving reality which is knowledge. Knowledge is over you through governance and you stand under the amount of knowledge you acquire. As your understanding expands, your ability to actuate that knowledge grows, resulting in wisdom. The term "power" refers to one's ability to act on knowledge, and those who perceive an exceptional creative ability to apply knowledge are often regarded as possessing genius.

One such moment of revelation came when the Word of God finally broke open in my heart. I had once believed that baptism in the name of the Father, Son, and Holy Ghost was sufficient. But it was the name of Jesus that pierced my spirit and revealed the true purpose of baptism: the remission of sins. After all, it was Jesus who bore the cross, it is Jesus' name that carries redemptive authority.

Years later, while driving downtown, my mind entered a state of meditation, and suddenly, God revealed to me the true purpose of the church. The revelation struck me with such force, as its obviousness became clear. It was the culmination of years of preaching and teaching, and in that moment, everything fell into place. I could hardly believe the depth of understanding I had received.

Several years later, while on a hill south of the city at dusk, I looked out over the city as street lights flickered on and buildings glowed. I realized they were all powered by the same grid. It became apparent that all these structures received power from the same source, the local energy company. In that moment, a profound revelation struck me: the Holy Ghost is the power source of the church, anointing, establishing, and empowering us for ministry, just as the streetlights and buildings in our cities are powered by the same electrical grid.

We must recognize that we are incapable of accomplishing anything apart from God, as the teachings of Christ clearly emphasize, He is the vine, and we are the branches. It is God who empowers us to fulfill

His will. As vessels created for His purpose, we possess no inherent power of our own. When God places us in a ministry, He grants us the power necessary to carry out that work. We remain empowered as long as God sustains us in that role, until He decides to bring about a change, which also makes King Saul a curious case.

<u>Anointed</u>

Leadership is not about giving directions; it is about leading and moving people in a direction. A leader must possess God's vision to move others in the right direction. Because it is a spiritual work, they are anointed to do so and to challenge the leader would be to challenge God. At the same time, God's people must be respected and empowered, as they belong to Him. We are all held accountable for our actions. While God rejected Saul due to his disobedience, Saul remained in a divinely established position, and David, who was also anointed, despite having the opportunity, dared not fight God and refrained from attacking the king. The role of king was established, ordained, and empowered by God. Eventually, David assumed this holy position after Saul's death. Though David had many personal flaws, he was anointed by God. God puts flawed humans in holy positions.

One can be anointed, and God is not with them. The anointing is God's establishment and empowerment of an individual for a divine purpose, and it is a necessary requirement for functioning in His service. No one brings the anointing. It comes from God. Continued service is contingent upon one's obedience to God. As demonstrated by figures like Lucifer, Saul, and many others, it is possible to choose to defy God even after He has sanctified you. The critical issue lies in the condition of your heart. If your heart is not perfect before God, if it is corrupted, God could reject you from His service, though the anointing may remain. In such cases, the individual will be held to a higher standard of accountability. Until we die, we are living with a terminal disease and that is the sin nature in our flesh.

The life of the church and a saint is the Holy Ghost. The Holy Ghost is God's spirit. Different types of anointing are given for various spiritual purposes. Without God's empowerment, the music ministry is ineffective and dead, regardless of the quality of the music. If not empowered by God, the music becomes a curse rather than a blessing. Ministry is sustained through God's power, working through His chosen vessels. Anointed is that which is established and the anointing is the divine power through that established designation. I call that power, a charge. The anointing cannot be earned; it is bestowed by God's will. And the glory of one ministry is not the same as another, even if they are similar. It is God who qualifies, not man. In His sovereignty, God selects and anoints individuals, often choosing those whom others may overlook or reject. Therefore, we should never give up on anyone, as we never know what God has planned for them.

You may witness someone thriving in their divine calling and quickly assume that, because you too are anointed, you can step into that same role-perhaps even outperform them. But being anointed alone does not guarantee success. If God has not appointed you to a specific task, even with being anointed, your efforts will fall flat. Take, for instance, a song leader. If God chooses someone else to lead a particular song, that person receives the grace and power, charge, needed for that exact moment. Because you too are a song leader, you may assume to minister in that same capacity. But without the same divine assignment, your endeavors will not produce the same spiritual impact. In fact, your efforts will be a curse. When people do not know God and this principle is misunderstood-especially in corrupt hearts, clouded by pride or spiritual immaturity-jealousy, rivalry, and division often take root, weakening the unity and effectiveness of the ministry as a whole.

The anointing also signifies God's approval, and our responsibility is to put in the effort to perfect the ministry, rather than leaving it as it is. Being anointed does not equate to perfection, but it signifies and established us in God's calling. The position of music ministry leader, often the minister of music, is an anointed role, and God alone determines who occupies it. The individual chosen for this position will be anointed and divinely protected.

Character

A doctor is not only defined by a certificate, nor is a police officer only considered a public servant simply by completing a ceremony. Similarly, ministry is not about practicing what you preach, but rather preaching what you practice. Your character is what truly qualifies you for service, rooted in the integrity and character you demonstrate.

James Burke made a series of bold, principled decisions that ultimately saved Johnson & Johnson from collapse. After seven people tragically died from consuming Tylenol capsules laced with cyanide, Burke ordered a nationwide recall of approximately 31 million bottles, a move that cost the company over $100 million. By prioritizing public safety and corporate transparency over immediate financial loss and potential damage to his own reputation, Burke demonstrated a deep commitment to the company's mission and long-term integrity.

In stark contrast, Stephen Elop's tenure at Nokia is often cited as a case study in corporate mismanagement. Once a global leader in mobile technology, Nokia's rapid decline under Elop's leadership is largely unknown to the general public. While Burke's decisions reflected a sense of purpose and vision, Elop's actions appeared more aligned with personal or internal interests, ultimately contributing to the company's downfall. These two CEOs illustrate how internal values define character. It's worth reflecting on a deeper truth: Why is it so easy to overlook the simplicity and power of what Jesus said, *"If you love me, keep my commandments"*?

You might carry the title of "minister," but do your actions reflect that role? The question is whether you truly embody what your title represents. The term "liar" is also someone whose character does not align with what they profess.

If ministry is going to be effective, God's power must be in it. We have become highly sophisticated in music creation, and we implement great creativity in production. Some of us have learned to refine our ministry and execute an advanced professional look and sound. Unfortunately, the emphasis has shifted from God-approved ministry to the reliance on sophisticated techniques and ideas as the standard. This trend must be reversed. While God certainly values professionalism, the essential prerequisite is the spirit and the anointing. We have in great excess wonderful sounding dead music. Music should sound great, but it is only ministry if it is charged by the power of God.

Heroes and cowards are defined by their actions. Through consistent obedience, a person is transformed, becoming who they were ultimately meant to be according to God's design. What you do establishes your life trajectory, and those choices should be guided by the principles found in God's word. However, we are often too preoccupied with the opinions of others, allowing external judgment to influence our direction rather than truth.

God did not establish the Church to function as a social club. Living by faith is an individualized and deeply personal journey between each person and God. Throughout the Bible, many of those whom

God used were not surrounded by crowds; instead, they were often rejected by friends and family, subjected to discrimination, and, in some cases, executed. Jesus made it clear that following Him comes at a cost, each believer must carry their cross. Therefore, we should not be surprised when trials and hardships arise. Early believers were called Christians because they followed Christ, who endured profound suffering, even unto death. Every Christian must be prepared to live according to their faith and to withstand the challenges it brings, including the possibility of persecution. Unfortunately, many in today's Church have lost sight of what it truly means to be a follower of Christ. Too often, the Church is treated as a source of entertainment, God is not vain.

A Christian will voluntarily surrender from their heart, anything and anyone, friends, family and even spouse for the Kingdom of God. They will do it because they are faith walkers, and they know God will take care of them, give them who they need, and they trust that God will perform every promise. A Christian is qualified for music ministry.

CHAPTER SIX

MINISTRY

And Saul sent to Jesse, saying, Let David, I pray thee, stand before me; for he hath found favour in my sight. And it came to pass, when the evil spirit from God was upon Saul, that David took an harp, and played with his hand: so Saul was refreshed, and was well, and the evil spirit departed from him.

1 Samuel 16:22-23 KJV

...for the joy of the LORD is your strength.
Nehemiah 8:10 KJV

Then one of them, which was a lawyer, asked him a question, tempting him, and saying, Master, which is the great commandment in the law?
Jesus said unto him, Thou shalt love the Lord thy God with all thy heart, and with all thy soul, and with all thy mind. This is the first and great commandment. And the second is like unto it, Thou shalt love thy neighbour as thyself. On these two commandments hang all the law and the prophets.
Matthew 22:35-40 KJV

And the spirits of the prophets are subject to the prophets. For God is not
the author of confusion, but of peace, as in all churches of the saints.
1 Corinthians 14:32-33 KJV

Is not this the fast that I have chosen? to loose the bands of wickedness,
to undo the heavy burdens, and to let the oppressed go free, and that ye
break every yoke?
Isaiah 58:6 KJV

The Condition

The nature of sound is spirit. While it's important for a vessel to be
physically healthy, spiritual health is even more crucial for effective
ministry, and spiritual health is defined by one's relationship with
God. Dominant spirits influence weaker ones, meaning that stronger
individuals have the ability to affect those who are weaker. We transmit
who we are. A leader must have a dominant spirit to influence others.
When ministering through music, the sound must be pure, as it's
presented before God's chosen people, who are the most valuable in
the earth. If our *spiritual condition* is corrupt, we risk disrupting the
ministry, as our corrupt spirit will negatively impact the ministry. A
struggling believer may still possess a pure heart, even if their actions
seem to contradict the teachings of the word. Musicians, including
singers, are those who create and lead others in music.

We often criticize society, lamenting how bad it has become. One
of the main reasons the world is in such turmoil is because too many
in the church are corrupt. We are the light of the world, the salt of
the earth. Now remember there are the saints in light and the saints in
darkness. A close reading of the first few chapters of *Revelation* reveals

that God took issue with the church. While the world is enslaved to sin and cannot save itself, the church holds the power on earth. However, the church has not always fulfilled the responsibility God entrusted to it. People have hijacked God's church and as a result, people around the world are suffering from unprecedented levels of violence and are seeking help. Many have turned to the church, hoping for solace.

When individuals attend a church service, they often come battered by life's hardships, crying out for help. So many personal struggles they face, and the devastation the world has caused them. One suicide is one too many, yet the statistics continue to rise. People are searching for help, but too often, they are dismissed as "too strange" to be worthy of salvation. However, no one but God can truly see the heart. Many of these individuals are rejected by society, desperately seeking love and purpose, while others are simply trying to navigate their way through life. The church is meant to be a sanctuary for the broken, but when these individuals arrive, what do they find?

We must recognize that everybody, everyone is navigating life while facing daily challenges and grappling with both internal and external matters, natural and spiritual. Pain is difficult to endure, and individuals cope with it in various ways, some of which may seem unusual, unfamiliar, distasteful or even wrong to others. People seek relief and are often willing to take any necessary, and sometimes seemingly unnecessary measures to alleviate their pain. It is too much! Judgment is a dangerous shortcut that bypasses compassion. This is why it is essential to stay in our own lane and refrain from passing judgment, as we are often unaware of the full complexity and nuances of others' experiences. Grief is a war. People we serve are not just looking for a song, they're looking for healing. Ultimately, we must remember that God is in control and fully aware of all things.

<u>Depression</u>

A condition is a holding state that governs the way something is. Altering the principle that causes the condition will change the condition. Depression is a condition that drives thoughts and behaviors. In contrast, being established in God and walking in His will produces a condition that produces a feeling of happiness. We call that condition, joy.

A powerful book I strongly recommend is *The Gospel of Mental Health* by Stacey McDonald. It offers profound insight into the intersection of faith and mental well-being. Clinical depression, in particular, is a serious and often misunderstood disorder. It manifests through persistent sadness, anxiety, numbness, and an absence of joy or interest in life. One of its most insidious effects is isolation. Depression often pushes individuals to withdraw inwardly, cutting them off from support and community. Without intervention, this isolation can spiral into deeper psychological darkness, even leading to suicidal thoughts or actions.

Though the causes of clinical depression vary widely, ranging from chemical imbalances to trauma, it is always a heavy burden. While depression is treatable, it cannot be dismissed as a mere weakness or something one can "snap out of." It is a complex mental state that requires understanding, care, and often professional support. Left untreated, its consequences can be devastating.

There are many mental health disorders that affect us and life presents challenges that can overwhelm even the strongest among us. Not everyone has the same mental or emotional capacity to cope with adversity. People respond to hardship in different ways and what one person manages with resilience, another may experience as emotionally crushing. That doesn't make them weak; it makes them human.

As believers, we are called to respond with compassion, not criticism. Many people around us are silently suffering, and some are genuinely helpless in the face of their battles. That's where the Church must rise. God has uniquely designed each life and, through the Church, offers healing, hope, and restoration. The Church isn't just a sanctuary for worship, it is a lifeline for the weary, a hospital for the broken, and a place of refuge for the mentally burdened.

Let us not be passive in the face of mental affliction. Let us be informed, deliberate, and compassionate, understanding that true ministry doesn't just speak to the spirit but ministers to the mind and heart as well.

Love

Love is not a fleeting emotion or a superficial feeling, it is a profound principle that dwells in the hidden chambers of the heart. It is the force behind our intentions, the silent driver of our decisions, and the essence that shapes how we live and relate to others. In today's world, love is often confused with lust and reduced to pleasure and physical gratification. Lust, at its core, is a corrupt desire, an appetite for sin masquerading as affection. Lust cannot evolve into love. By nature, it is self-serving and destructive. Those who give in to it risk surrendering their will and violating the commandments of God.

Scripture, particularly in the book of *James*, speaks clearly on this. Lust, when conceived, gives birth to sin; and sin, when it is finished, brings forth death. God, who *is* love, gave us commandments not to restrict us, but to preserve us. These divine boundaries protect the soul, and when we cross them, we expose ourselves to grave consequences. *"For the wages of sin is death..."*

Many of us profess to love God and identify as followers of Christ, but the real question is: *Do our lives reflect Christ?* Jesus instructed that rich man to sell all his possessions and follow him, but the man's heart was bound to his wealth, preventing him from obedience. Jesus wasn't asking for a donation; He was testing the man's heart. Likewise, we are called to *seek first* the Kingdom of God. Everything else, status, relationships, material wealth, will one day fade. What remains is our spirit and its eternal destination.

If your heart is anchored in God's purpose, He will take care of the rest. But what is holding your heart hostage? What hidden attachments are keeping you from full obedience?

Love covers a multitude of sins. And yet, how easily we harbor resentment, division, and selfishness. We claim to love, but where is our compassion? Our patience? Our humility? If Jesus walked among us today, He would not just preach love, He would live it. And if our lives are not drawing others to Him, then we must ask: What value are we really offering?

Christ called us the *salt of the earth.* But salt that loses its savor is good for nothing. If you've repented, been baptized in the name of Jesus for the remission of sins, and received the Holy Ghost, yet refuse to fully submit to His word, you are taking His name in vain. Vanity is without purpose. Disobedience, even in small things, can lead us down a destructive path.

God's people are called to live by love. But here's a deeper question: *Do you love yourself?* Because true love begins within. Many of us wrestle with guilt, shame, and inner criticism. We're human, flawed, vulnerable, and often broken. Holiness is not the absence of mistakes; it's a life set apart for God. And while we can't achieve absolute perfection in these mortal bodies, the Bible defines perfection as *spiritual maturity,* a heart that seeks God's will and lives accordingly.

You will stumble. You will fall. But that doesn't disqualify you. In fact, God often uses those who have fallen the hardest to minister with the greatest depth. The fall is not the end, it's often the beginning of deeper grace.

At the same time, we must also recognize that the world is spiritually lost and influenced by forces that promote confusion while deception and sin have clouded the hearts and minds of many. People wander without direction, often unaware of how lost they truly are. This is the human condition under the curse of sin. But salvation, the great gift of God, is the remedy. And we, as His people, are called to carry this message of hope with urgency and compassion remembering *Proverbs 11:30* deep within our hearts.

Even in cultural traditions there is opportunity. While it's widely known that Jesus was not born on December 25, the global acknowledgment of His birth during that season is still significant. In a world that ignores God for most of the year, we must not dismiss the one time the world turns its eyes, even briefly, toward Christ. It's not about the date; it's about the *door*. Rather than criticize, let us capitalize on the moment and use it to point people toward eternal truth.

Effective ministry requires wisdom, patience, and above all, empathy. We must meet people where they are. Without trust, there can be no transformation. People won't listen until they know they're loved. Correction without relationship breeds resistance. But when ministry is rooted in love, compassion, and understanding, it becomes a lifeline, and lives begin to change.

Obedience

When Jesus healed ten lepers, He didn't touch them on the spot. Instead, He gave them a command: *"Go, show yourselves to the priest."* It was **as they went,** in obedience, that they were healed. Their break-through came not from standing still, but from stepping forward in faith.

This moment reveals something powerful: personal issues don't disqualify you from serving God. In fact, they should help fuel your faith. Every believer no matter their past or present struggles, has a place in God's work. Even those in high positions face trials. Yet many disqualify themselves, believing they aren't "spiritual enough" to be used. But your spiritual walk is not measured by how you feel; it is anchored in faith as demonstrated in *Habakkuk* and *Hebrews*.

The key is obedience. Engage your calling. Move in your assign-ment. And trust that God will meet you as you go. You cannot cleanse or prepare yourself on your own. Transformation is a divine work. Re-member Saul: he was chosen while still en route to persecute Chris-tians. God called him, not when he was ready, but when God decided he was ready.

The nervous system transmits messages throughout the body to trigger an immediate response. However, there are times when the nervous system fails to function properly, preventing these messages from reaching their intended destination. Conditions that impair the nervous system in this way are known as neurodegenerative disorders. Obedience to God should be an immediate response. Slothfulness is unrighteous because God's power is intended for prompt action. One cannot receive blessings if God is not a priority in their life. God's power is not casual. It's active, urgent, and purposeful. Love, not obligation, should drive our obedience from the heart.

Partial obedience, however, is not obedience at all. *1 Samuel 15* makes this painfully clear. Saul obeyed, *partially,* and it cost him everything. God doesn't accept selective compliance. If we obey in nine areas but reject one, it is still disobedience. As *James* reminds us, to break even a single point of God's law is to fall short of it entirely. God desires full surrender, not half-hearted attempts.

Slothfulness has no place in the Church. Everything under heaven has a time and season, which means your calling has a divine appointment. Delaying your response is not just procrastination, it's rebellion. When God calls, it's your *moment*. If you refuse, delay, or shrink back in fear, you risk forfeiting your place. I have personally seen God replace those who allowed laziness and disobedience to rob them of their assignment. God gives doors of opportunity, but doors do not stay open forever.

Never assume God *needs* you. He is the most creative Being. He will accomplish His will with or without your participation. Those who refuse to prepare, invest, or commit will not walk in the fullness of their calling. Consider the parable of the talents: faithful stewardship is the measure of success. And in music ministry especially, passion must be rooted in the heart. For some, your sound may be their first encounter with the presence of God.

God alone appoints and assigns. When He gives you a purpose, no one can steal it, but you can forfeit it through neglect or fear. He grows angry not at weakness, but at those who refuse to take ownership of their divine calling. Many are bound by fear, shame, or low self-worth, forgetting that none of us are worthy. Yet we are chosen, redeemed, and called with purpose. To act on your belief that you are not ready, when God has already chosen you, is to question His wisdom, and is rebellion in disguise. But without faith...

And beware, seeking validation from people can be fatal to your calling. Those around you may not understand what God is doing in your life. Some will question you. Others, driven by jealousy or fear, may oppose you. But when God places something in your spirit, you must act with boldness and urgency. The enemy loves to use familiar voices to create doubt and distraction. If your focus is not fixed on God's direction, you will lose your way.

This is not the time to hesitate. This is not the season to delay. God has called you, now. He has already equipped you. Move forward in faith. Trust that He will sustain you as you go.

Ministry

In most church services, music is the first element that ushers the congregation into the presence of God. It calms minds, prepares hearts, changes spirits, and sets the spiritual tone for the delivery of the living Word. Music ministry is spiritual work. It must reach the wounded, soothe the weary, and guide people toward Christ.

If you are not a vessel of love, you do not belong in music ministry. If your gifts are tainted with pride, bitterness, or a spirit of darkness, you do not belong in music ministry.
If you cannot respect your fellow ministers, you do not belong in music ministry.
The issue is not talent—it is the heart.

So, what is the vision for the music ministry?

Like any successful organization, a music ministry must have a clear and purposeful direction. Its sound and ministry should reflect the spiritual identity and depth of the local church. Anointing must come first, skill second. Don't expect a structure to stand firm if there is no foundation.

Ministry is, at its core, about connection. Yet, for many, the church experience feels disconnected, as if the service is a show rather than a sacred encounter. People may enjoy the music, sit through the sermon, and then leave unchanged. That is not ministry; that is entertainment. Entertainment amuses. Ministry awakens. It revives. The purpose of the Church is not to impress but to elevate the soul and lead people to God.

God gives gifts and anoints people for the unique purpose He designed them to fulfill. As the late Bishop Jeremiah Reed once said: *"If you don't do what God has called you to do, He has nothing else for you to do."* Ministry requires growth, refinement, and humility. No one is without flaws or possesses all the answers. It's not magic, it's a process.

There must be balance in all things. Zeal without order leads to confusion. Excitement is good, but it must be tempered by discipline. Remember, people come to church seeking something real. The music ministry exists to serve *them*. And service requires awareness. I've seen worship leaders become so caught up in the experience that they leave the congregation behind. If the people are not engaged, we have failed to minister. Ministry is also about mutual participation.

In our nursing home ministry, I witnessed a powerful example of this. When we sang unfamiliar songs, the residents appreciated the sound, but something was missing. There wasn't much of a connection. But the moment we sang something familiar, they lit up. They sang. They smiled. They worshiped. We were unified. That's the heart of music ministry, to unify, to include, to bring people in. While we may not always be able to communicate verbally, singing together allows us to connect in a profound way. And if the congregation doesn't know the song? Then it is your ministry to *teach* it. Give them a song.

Music must do more than sound good, it must facilitate a breakthrough. The atmosphere in any service can vary. Some moments are heavy with spiritual resistance. In those moments, anointed music becomes the battering ram. But this requires deep sensitivity to the Spirit. Worship leaders must know when to linger, when to shift, when to speak, and when to be silent. Each person carries a unique burden, and the Spirit of God knows every emotional and mental state in the room. A song held too long can lose its power. A song cut short can stifle a breakthrough. The goal is not to finish a setlist, it is to follow God.

When the spirit is in the song, it should be carried to its fullest expression before transitioning to the next phase of the service. Choir directors and song leaders must be sensitive to the spirit, sensing when to continue and when to shift. All musicians must be able to connect with God.

And no, this does not give us permission to lose control. Emotions are natural, but we are still called to order. God is not chaotic. Our passion must be guided by wisdom. I urge musicians, those who play instruments and singers alike, when the energy rises, discipline must rise with it. Enthusiasm is beautiful, but skill, prayer, and preparation are the tools to direct that energy with excellence. That is why consistent practice is indispensable.

The music ministry is not about showcasing your ability.
It's about stewarding your gift.
It's about reaching people through sound, through song, and through Spirit.
It's about love.

So before you take the stage, ask yourself: *Is my heart in the right place?*
Because the atmosphere you shape may be the very gateway through which someone meets God.

<u>Leadership</u>

As previously mentioned, the question remains: *What is the vision for the music ministry?* It must be engineered and organized, prepared not just for services, but for *ministry*. Preparation is the foundation of effectiveness and the key to success. When the Spirit moves, the ministry must be ready to respond, not scrambling, not stalling, but poised, alert, and ready to go.

You should be prepared for any service or event, never caught off guard. Build a comprehensive and well-rehearsed repertoire, beginning with songs requested by the pastor and expanding to those that resonate most with the congregation. This not only creates unity but allows the Holy Ghost to flow freely, inspiring the right song at the right moment, and allowing you to execute it with excellence, not hesitation.

Leadership and delegation are critical. Leaders must assign roles clearly and create an atmosphere of clarity and accountability. Draft a detailed document that outlines the ministry's vision, mission, and goals. Define each position, its responsibilities, and expectations so that every team member knows their role and understands how their part fits into God's greater plan.

Accountability cannot be compromised. Every participant must be reliable and informed, knowing when, where, and how they are expected to serve. Absences without communication disrupt the flow of ministry and diminish its effectiveness. God's work demands faithfulness. Those who repeatedly fail to honor their commitments are not yet ready to serve at the level ministry requires. Inconsistency is not just inconvenient, it can be spiritually costly.

Everyone involved must understand the vision, embrace it as their own, and give themselves fully to it. When people love what they do, they prepare, they show up, and they serve with passion. As a leader, surround yourself with people who not only support you but challenge you constructively. Agreement does not always indicate alignment, and disagreement doesn't always mean disloyalty. Just because your position is correct does not necessarily mean your direction is. Therefore, mutual respect must be maintained among all parties.

It is imperative for leaders to dedicate personal time to communion with God. Consistent periods of private devotion and prayer are essential for cultivating a deep and authentic relationship with the Creator. Spiritual leaders must actively seek the mind of God and maintain mental and spiritual clarity, particularly when entrusted with guiding others in His work. Distractions can significantly impede the discernment required to hear and follow God's direction. Moreover, God has entrusted leaders with a voice that influences those under their care. Therefore, sustained fellowship with God not only enhances a leader's capacity to be attuned to the Spirit's guidance in ministry but also enables them to lead by example and mentor those they serve. In this context, it is vital that the heart of the leader is genuinely aligned with the music ministry, as authentic leadership begins with internal conviction and spiritual alignment.

The music ministry must also be in the hearts of all those involved. If the music ministry is truly in their hearts, there would be no need for speeches to remind them of how grateful they should be to serve in the music ministry. They would already understand the honor of being in God's service. Musicians should be thankful for the opportunity to sing and play God's praises before His people, regardless of personal circumstances. All should minister from the depths of their souls. Failing to do so is a disservice to themselves and hinders the ministry. Moreover, the spirit from the pulpit must exceed that of the congregation.

The pulpit must lead the pew. The spirit, energy, and reverence of those ministering should surpass that of the congregation. A cold ministry will never ignite a burning heart. Ministry must flow from the soul, not just from talent.

But even passion must be refined. Training is essential. Invest in your craft. Take lessons. Learn your instrument. Study vocal technique. Understand your body and how it functions in service and in sound. A natural gift is powerful, but untrained talent is limited in its reach. If your aim is to give God your best, then seek knowledge, seek discipline, and pursue growth. God gave His best. He expects no less from us.

And remember this principle: *The one who works gets paid.* Those who labor faithfully in God's house will never be overlooked by the One who sees in secret. The return may not always be financial, but it will always be divine.

Practice

Etiquette in all its forms must be consistent and practiced. Sing with clarity and control, not by overpowering the room with volume. Play your instrument with precision, not with force. Cultivate a strong, confident stage presence, and always carry yourself with grace and professionalism, especially when in the presence of others. This is ministry, and with that calling comes a higher standard.

You are not ordinary. God has elevated you for His divine purpose. That means you must rise to the level He has assigned, not the level your comfort or insecurities suggest. Doubt must be cast off completely. If God called you, He has equipped you, and He is depending on you.

Excellence is not spontaneous. It is forged through deliberate practice. The principle of mastery is timeless. No one becomes great by accident. The "10,000-hour rule" is more than a theory, it is a powerful reminder that skill is sharpened by repetition, and greatness is born from consistency, not convenience. While natural talent is beneficial, the story of basketball legend Michael Jordan exemplifies that it is consistent effort and hard work that lead to triumph. Mistakes are not setbacks; they are stepping stones. It's not "perfect practice" that propels you, rather, it's persistent, thoughtful practice over time. Mastery in music, as in any field, is not achieved through magic, but through persistent practice, both during and after reaching greatness.

The one who works gets paid.

Remember, there is a difference between possessing information and embodying knowledge. To truly connect with music, you must internalize it. This is the fundamental purpose of practice. You don't just master a song, you become it. You must internalize the music so deeply that it's like a natural extension of you, something you can skillfully wield in service of ministry.

This is the true aim of practice: to transform information into embodiment, skill into instinct, and performance into worship. When every member of a music ministry reaches this level of engagement, the group moves as one. The ministry becomes synchronized, seamless, and through that harmony, God moves more powerfully. Without preparation, however, that deeper emotional and spiritual connection remains out of reach.

Practice is where the foundation is laid. Rehearsal, however, is different. Rehearsal is where what you've already mastered in private is brought into alignment with others. You should not come to rehearsal to learn the material, you should arrive ready to build with the team. Rehearsals must be focused, structured, and efficient. Every participant should arrive prepared, punctual, and present in both body and spirit.

We must also be sensitive to God's direction in song selection. When God chooses a song, we do not discard it simply because we've grown tired of it. At our church, the altar call song has remained the same for years, not because of tradition, but because God has not yet said to change it. He knows what His people need. Personal preference and musical ambition must never override divine instruction.

Too often, we veer off course, not from outright rebellion, but from spiritual neglect. Prayer has waned. Fasting has faded. And as a result, we lose sensitivity to the Spirit's leading. Our ability to discern what God wants from the music ministry is rooted in our spiritual life, not just our musical skill.

Names sanction a character. Latin names are given in biology to describe what it is based on its characteristics. Those in the music ministry should internalize the message of *Mark 11:17*. We make time for what we value. If you are not praying in the house of God consistently, barring unavoidable life situations, then you must ask: *Is your spiritual life operating the way it should?* Ministry requires more than talent. It requires commitment. And above all, it requires intimacy with God.

The Priesthood

Fasting is a deliberate act of discipline that brings the flesh into submission. In a world that encourages indulgence, fasting also reminds us that self-control is imperative for the believer. It also helps to bring you to your spiritual baseline and an aid against mind fights. Fast in faith with purpose.

God is willing to act, but not without your participation. Many cry out, "Lord, help me!"-yet fail to examine their own responsibility in the matter. What are you doing? Too often, Christians overlook a crucial truth: they wait for God to "fix" situations He has already given them the authority and power to address. Yes, God performs miracles, but He also calls us to partner with His Spirit in shaping our character.

The Holy Ghost is not a passive possession. It's an active force meant to guide our decisions. If you "put your Holy Ghost on a shelf," don't be surprised when your life reflects that distance. Every choice we make carries weight, blessings for obedience, consequences for compromise. Scripture commands us not to let sin reign in our bodies, and whether or not it does is ultimately a choice. The Holy Ghost enables us to live above sin, not beneath its influence.

It was forbidden for the people to approach God directly under the Old Testament, the Levites served as intermediaries, going to God on behalf of the people. This was the role of the priest. However, under the New Testament, God has moved His people into the priesthood, allowing saints to approach Him directly. This privilege, often neglected by many saints, remains the most powerful weapon in the church. The enemy may fight a praise service but will war against a prayer service. Why? Because prayer moves God, shifts the atmosphere, tears down strongholds, and strengthens our connection to God. It also helps to reorient your thought process. If you are not a person of prayer, your music ministry will lack power, no matter how skilled you are. Music has always been present on the battlefield, but when combined with fasting and prayer, it becomes a very powerful weapon of spiritual warfare.

Consider the hymn *"What a Friend We Have in Jesus."* This song should resonate deeply with anyone called to minister through music. It reminds us that prayer is not only communication, or just exchanging information, it is communion. Prayer attunes your spirit to God. It humbles you, silences ego, and makes space for the Spirit to move. When you consistently connect with the source of love, transformation is inevitable. And from that place, music becomes ministry.

Spirituality

The most effective way to defeat an enemy is to understand that enemy. Our adversary is no amateur and he is well-acquainted with church culture and masterful in his strategy. His primary weapon is distraction. He doesn't need to destroy you; he only needs to divert your focus. It's dangerously easy to become so caught up in spiritual routine that we fail to realize we are operating on empty. Like the Israelites of old, who continued their rituals unaware that the power of God had departed, we can fall into the trap of assuming that activity equals intimacy. Samson didn't even realize the Lord had left him. Neither the Children of Israel when they attacked Ai. Likewise, many believers continue functioning without the presence of God, mistaking blessings for confirmation. But not every blessing is a sign of divine approval.

The Christian walk is not measured by natural success. Some of us may endure sickness, disability, or struggle, not because of a lack of faith, but by divine design. True blessing is spiritual, and no amount of wealth, status, or human connection can replace a relationship with God. In fact, the very things we cherish, careers, families, friendships, can become distractions if they take precedence over our relationship with Him. Your relationship with God is deeply personal, and some have faced the difficult choice between prioritizing their relationships or God. However, God must remain the primary focus in your life, for He is the source of all life. Everyone involved in music ministry must make God their priority. When you allow God to guide your life, you will become an offense to some people, and as a result, lose friends and family. As you continue to follow God in obedience, you will eventually enter what I heard from Bishop Dwight A. Reed of Christ Apostolic Temple to be your "wilderness period."

John 8:32 is a process. Trials work to break the power and influence of the flesh, allowing the Spirit of God greater access to operate through you as you voluntarily submit to a spirit of humility, all accomplished through the power of faith. Furthermore, all trials are designed to strengthen and build our faith. While the reality of clinical depression and the fact that life can be incredibly difficult, especially for those battling severe mental health challenges, I still believe that God is able to deliver. At the same time, what I would like to emphasize is the attitude we must adopt in order to sustain our ministry. We cannot overlook our personal responsibility in the face of hardship. When David's own men turned against him and sought to take his life, their reaction was understandable given the extreme circumstances. Yet, David chose to encourage himself, seek the mind of God, and ultimately prevail. Do we truly recognize who we are?

All musicians should carry Psalm 100 deeply in their hearts. Life presents challenges to everyone, and we do not have the luxury of viewing ourselves as exceptions simply because circumstances did not unfold in our favor. Self-centeredness, often masked as discouragement, is rooted in unbelief. Without embodying the fruits of the Spirit, we cannot minister effectively.

Experience induces knowledge and adds credibility and substance to your character. A key feature of sanctification is knowing God through experience. The wilderness period is a pivotal phase in a Christian's life, where God strips away everything and everyone, leaving you alone with Him. During this time, some may judge or reject you, while others may deem you incapable of overcoming. Your faith is tested in ways unlike any other time in your life. This is a moment of spiritual truth and rebirth, where, like the caterpillar transforming into a butterfly, you are made new. Successfully navigating this trial elevates your Christian walk, enabling you to receive a higher level of anointing and increasing your effectiveness in spiritual warfare. However, without a genuine desire to serve God, you will not endure. You may not always understand or appreciate your circumstances, but trust that God has already worked everything out for your good. God will always deliver.

The stories of Abraham, Joseph, Job, and many others in the bible are not hyperbole. These were real people who faced genuine challenges, and their testimonies serve as powerful examples meant to strengthen our faith. God is not intent on destroying us and many of us find ourselves in situations where we begin to question God and even His existence.

However, when you get to where you actually know God, and that takes a lot of time and experience, then you will understand that all of it is for His sake and because you represent Him as a witness in this earth, if you remain in His will, He will not let you fall. Just as loving parents prepare their children for success, God even more so equips us for His work in the world. This imparts tremendous value to our lives, yet it remains essential to make wise choices-because while God has a plan for each of us, He is never without alternatives. It is a battle, a spiritual battle in the mind.

Music plays a crucial role on the battlefield. As musicians and ministers, we have a responsibility to be prepared at all times. Regardless of what is happening in our personal lives or the atmosphere of the congregation, we must be ready to serve God at a moment's notice. It is not the responsibility of others to motivate or activate us. We must leave our personal struggles behind, set aside any negative attitudes, and work together. When the time comes to minister, we must offer our best to God. Consistently giving our best, even when faced with challenges, will naturally reflect in our ministry, and this is precisely what God desires.

As we minister to others, it is essential that we first attend to our own spiritual well-being. Speaking words of life over oneself, through prayer and affirmations, is a vital practice. Just as those empowered by the Holy Spirit through the priesthood may lay hands in blessing, so too must we not neglect ourselves in this sacred responsibility. Lay hands on yourself. It is our responsibility alone to care for our vessel. While communal prayer and mutual support are important, neglecting your spiritual health is negligence in ministry.

For many, it is challenging to be as faithful as God calls us to be because we often fail to consistently show up for God. We cannot be successful in God serving Him from an obligatory perspective. It must be from the standpoint of love. We must get to the place where we let it all go. Until then we will always be handicapped. If we are truly going to "let God arise," we must stop aligning with the enemy and surrender our flesh, choosing instead to work together in unity and love. This raises an important question: Do you truly believe in God as you profess?

Obligation Versus Love

The music ministry, like all work done for God, requires complete dedication. Let us examine several key traits that determine whether we, as saints, are in proper or improper standing in fulfilling the responsibilities of the music ministry. Do you serve God out of a sense of obligation, fulfilling your duties simply because they must be completed? Or do you serve out of love, driven by deep affection, excitement, and genuine concern for the vision? Let's evaluate one's state of being when serving from the positions of obligation and love.

I. SERVING FROM OBLIGATION

-Motivation

1. Extrinsically driven motivation, fear of consequences, pressure

2. Focus on duty not vision

3. Will not be proactive or go beyond what is asked of them

-Energy & Engagement

1. Feels drained or indifferent or forced

2. Frequently checks the clock

3. Looks for distractions

-Creativity & Initiative

1. Avoids extra responsibility

2. Resists change, resistance to growth

-Quality of Work

1. May be rushed, inconsistent of just "good enough."

-Emotional State

1. More Prone to stress, frustration, and burnout

2. May look for external validation

3. Rigid attitude

4. Complaining

5. Lack of joy

-Relationships

1. May feel isolated, resentful, or disconnected from peers

II. SERVING FROM LOVE

-Motivation

1. Intrinsically motivated

2. Has a deep connection with purpose and vision, committed to the mission

3. Driven by curiosity and fulfillment

4. Carries a spirit of sacrifice

-Energy & Engagement

1. Feels energized, immersed in their work, loss of track of time

2. Interest in investing more time and energy

3. Strong attitude of perseverance

-Creativity & Initiative

1. Brings new ideas, seeks growth, takes self-initiative

2. Eagerness and willingness to grow and expand

3. Interested in enhancing their skills

-Quality of Work

1. Produces higher quality work, more thoughtful and consistent results

2. Puts in the extra effort and care

-Emotional State

1. More positive, optimistic, and resilient in changes

2. Has a positive attitude and a spirit of gratitude

3. Maintains a spirit of joy

-Relationships

1. Builds strong and positive connections, collaborates well, uplifts others

2. Values others and their thoughts and opinions

While it may be easy to scrutinize others, doing so often comes at our own expense. A more mature and responsible approach is to begin with self-examination before assigning blame elsewhere. Regardless of who may be at fault, our first response should be to bring the matter, and the individual, before God in prayer. The principles rooted in our hearts ultimately shape our actions, which is why we must ask ourselves the hard questions: *Is there anything within me that may be hindering the ministry?* True growth begins not with critique, but with honest reflection.

Disillusioned

Many once walked in belief, but when the spirit of deception takes root, the path back to truth becomes increasingly narrow. In a world obsessed with self-advancement, we often prioritize natural success, chasing wealth, recognition, and influence by offering our gifts to secular pursuits. Meanwhile, satanic forces hide the consequences behind a polished illusion, offering empty promises that captivate the heart and distort the mind. Many have been lured into this deception, convinced that the grass is greener on the other side. But ask yourself: *Can the world truly offer more than God?*

If God is the author of time, is His timing not perfect? We proclaim Him as our refuge and strength, a present help in trouble, yet we often resist the discipline of waiting on Him. Is He not sovereign? Has His authority changed?

God is always working behind the scenes, orchestrating events for our good. Our trust must be anchored in His word, not in our feelings, not in the opinions of others, and certainly not in the fear of delay. Time, when surrendered to God, is always on our side. Yet, many turn away, seeking fulfillment elsewhere, believing their moment has passed, if it ever came. But no one holds power within themselves, not even the power to return to God on their own terms. Departure from His presence is not always followed by a return. What, then, is the congregation of the dead?

CHAPTER SEVEN

MUSIC

And Chenaniah, chief of the Levites, was for song: he instructed about the song, because he was skilful.
1 Chronicles 15:22 KJV

All these were under the hands of their father for song in the house of the LORD, with cymbals, psalteries, and harps, for the service of the house of God, according to the king's order to Asaph, Jeduthun, and Heman. So the number of them, with their brethren that were instructed in the songs of the LORD, even all that were cunning, was two hundred fourscore and eight.
1 Chronicles 25:6-7 KJV

Sing unto him a new song; play skillfully with a loud noise.
Psalms 33:3 KJV

The Purpose of the Music Ministry

Another recommended book is *This Is Your Brain on Music: The Science of a Human Obsession* by Daniel J. Levitin. The purpose of music in the church is to transform the spirits of the congregation by creating a spiritual and emotional connection through the atmosphere, thereby preparing their minds to receive the word of God. God utilizes a lead minister or ministers to guide the service, or event, or occasion, directing the congregation's or participant's focus toward Him. The life of the ministry, the spirit of God, the Holy Ghost, anoints and empowers individuals for ministry. It is the spiritual force that enables listeners to be prepared to receive the living word. Anointed music alters the atmosphere, touches the souls, and elevates the mind, ultimately opening the heart. When the heart is open, it becomes ready to receive the word of God.

Music played a crucial role in warfare, serving functions such as communication, morale enhancement, intimidation, and participation in rituals and ceremonies. This is spiritual warfare and we must position the most skilled individuals at the forefront while simultaneously preparing and empowering others to assume leadership roles in the future.

Notice how proficiency is a demand in God's word. Training is essential for any endeavor, and the music ministry is no exception. Music has such a profound impact that those involved must be knowledgeable and skilled in their craft. If you sing, you should understand your body and how to use it properly to avoid damaging your voice. Regardless of the instrument you play, it is crucial to know how to use and maintain it effectively, as well as how to teach others. True proficiency as a musician is also demonstrated by your ability to pass on your knowledge to others.

In ancient Israel, those entering music ministry underwent at least five years of training, a testament to the seriousness with which their role was regarded. The same principle applies today: if we fail to plan, we plan to fail. People place their faith in the music ministry to deliver, and if you find yourself at the same level as the previous year, you are not investing in your ministry. Continuous growth is essential. The church must cultivate a musical culture that prioritizes ongoing learning, practice, composition, and production, always preparing to be used by God.

Society turns to musicians for escape, connection, and identity. Celebrity musicians attract massive followings due to their personal brand and the values they are perceived to represent. Their influence is so powerful that it plays a significant role in driving the global economy.

Music is ubiquitous, found everywhere you go. A friend of mine, for instance, was a musician even while in prison. Music carries such immense spiritual weight, which is why we must be deliberate and thoughtful about how we incorporate it into church services and events. While every ministry may have its own approach, it's crucial to understand why people come to church and the role music plays in that experience.

Ministry is fundamentally about connection, first to God, and then to others, and the music ministry, in particular, relies on this connection. Too many musicians have lost their connection with God, and as a result, they become disconnected from the very people they are called to serve. Music ministry is a mission. That mission is salvation. It is about leading people into the mindset to receive God and, ultimately, changing lives. While ideas and strategies have their place, Scripture reminds us that "unless the Lord builds the house, they labor in vain who build it." It is not about great ideas, but about the power of God.

The church is distinct from the world, and the world is not meant to define the church. If individuals cannot find what they need within the church, why would they choose to come? There must be a clear distinction. So many People have lost their connection to the church, indicating that the church has not always fulfilled its intended purpose. Salvation is about deliverance from the world, and for the church to fulfill its mission, it cannot conform to worldly standards. If we are vessels, it is not we who reach out to young people, but God using us to do so. If we are not careful, we may miss the message He intends to convey. Young people are new to the scene and need guidance and teaching. They should always feel free to contribute in any way they wish, but this should be done under proper guidance. The orderly approach is for directions to come from the top down.

Music is out front. As leaders, we carry the responsibility of setting an example. We are admired for our ministry, and many look to us to embody honesty and integrity in our Christian walk. Our influence is significant, and our presence carries weight. God desires to work through us, but how can He when we are distracted, consumed by pride from constant praise, or disgraced because of our faithlessness? Ours is a dangerous ministry; a misstep on our part can impact many, and God holds us accountable for the consequences. We have nothing to offer God except our full surrender and total commitment. We are told we have nothing but filthy rags. If we are to be of any true value, we must be wholly committed, mind, body, and spirit, to the God who called us.

Deception

The word speaks about a haughty spirit, and as musicians, uniquely gifted by God, we must remain especially vigilant. Music wields extraordinary influence over the human mind, particularly when paired with the right message. We see this dynamic clearly in culture: artists often shape public opinion, identity, and values. The entertainment industry understands this power and capitalizes on it. Media platforms and social networks are saturated with influencers and fans who elevate these figures, feeding an ever-growing cycle of influence and idolatry.

Take special notice at *2 Corinthians 10:5*. The fall of Lucifer occurred because he thought more highly of himself than he should have. His story is a cautionary tale, echoed in *Romans 12:3*, reminding us not to think more highly of ourselves than we ought. As musicians, it is easy to lose sight of God's will when we become overly focused on our abilities, whether in singing, producing, writing, or anything else. These gifts, given by God for His glory, can be distorted when used to build our own platforms rather than His kingdom. What may feel like ministry becomes self-expression without submission. We must remember: we are not here to entertain or perform, we are here to fulfill God's purpose.

The enemy often seduces through the illusion of pleasure, wealth, and worldly success, hiding the steep price of that lifestyle. Scripture is clear that some of God's most faithful servants were wealthy, but their prosperity came from alignment with His will, not deviation from it. In reality, the reason many saints do not experience financial prosperity is due to a lack of understanding about the purpose of money and how to manage it. God's people are His work and testimony, which makes it more logical for a believer to be prosperous than to live in poverty. There is no need to misappropriate your gifts by offering them to the world for any reason. The enemy sets many traps, and unfortunately, many saints have fallen into them. If you stray from God, you may find it difficult, if not impossible, to return.

God desires for us to prosper greatly, but He first wants His people to be individuals of substance. One reason many saints do not qualify for certain blessings is that they have not matured enough to handle them, and many seek things that God does not intend for them to have. Remember, God always has our best interests at heart. We have a natural tendency to lean toward our own destruction, yet God has an incredible life in store for us, one that many would find hard to believe. However, we can only reach that life by remaining in His will. Patience, endurance, and commitment of time are essential to this journey.

Never forget what the word says about time and seasons. Some ministries take longer to develop, while others may grow more quickly. Never rely solely on your feelings, but instead on what you know. Trusting in the Lord comes with experience. This walk with Christ is not for the faint of heart; it is a battle, and the battlefield is your mind. The saying says, "An idle mind is the devil's workshop." So what is your mind processing?

You bear the sole responsibility of protecting your mind. Learn to wait on the Lord, He will act, but in His time, not yours. It is easy to self-destruct when we fail to develop the discipline and patience to stand still and allow God to work. Remember, God runs the show. We know there are people who worship the devil. God runs the devil.

Take heed of the "way that seems right." Scripture is written for and about spiritual people. The "broad way" does not simply refer to the world; it represents saints who interpret their Christian walk through a carnal mindset. It appears wise, even righteous, but it leads to destruction. Too often, we are so consumed by external circumstances that we miss God's voice because we lack spiritual sensitivity. Many musicians do not maintain a consistent prayer life, and this spiritual disconnection carries real consequences. That's why we need God's vision. Without it, even the most gifted among us drift. And yes, when we speak of musicians, we include singers, whether or not they play an instrument.

We are the sum of our experiences, and our decisions are often informed by our past. The purpose of the word is to revive us, renew our minds, cleanse our thoughts and hearts, and instruct us in how to live a life pleasing to God, while recreating Himself in us. But in our emotional fits, we cast aside the word, convinced that we can find our own solutions. In times of mental anguish, some even declare, "Church is no longer for me." Many saints today are spiritually bankrupt, struggling with faith and disconnected.

Everyone has a purpose. In my journey to discover mine, I was often told to "do what you love." Over time, I realized that true purpose lies at the intersection of what you love and what you are gifted at. Through prayer and time God will reveal that to you. My pastor introduced me to the concept of a purpose-driven life, one in which purpose takes the driver's seat, helping to guide me in every decision and direction. Until you begin to operate within your God-given purpose, you will always feel a sense of dissatisfaction.

For some, the music ministry serves as their first encounter with God. Even if that's not the case, consider this: How do you represent Him? What does your prayer life look like? Where does your faith stand? Do you truly love your neighbor as yourself? Are you striving to live in obedience to God's Word to the best of your ability? We are all at different points in our spiritual journey, and while you may be facing serious challenges, if you are giving your sincere effort, that is enough—God honors that. Be authentic. Embrace who you are, flaws and all, because God already has. But above all, never quit. Never give up. Keep pressing forward. Keep going and when you have done all....

The Sound Ministry

It's vital to recognize that while the music ministry and sound ministry serve distinct purposes, they are deeply interconnected. Each has its own role within the worship experience, but when these ministries work together in unity, they create something far greater than the sum of their parts. A strong, collaborative relationship between the two is essential for delivering a worship experience that is both impactful and spiritually cohesive.

Musicians benefit immensely from gaining a basic understanding of sound engineering. This shared knowledge fosters clearer communication, reduces misunderstandings, and builds mutual respect. As trust grows, alongside awareness of each other's working styles and personalities, tension fades. There should be no conflict between the two, because ultimately, both are striving toward the same goal: bringing souls to the Lord Jesus Christ.

The role of a sound engineer is far more than simply adjusting volume levels. It requires a discerning ear, a strong grasp of acoustic dynamics, and the ability to create a balanced mix that supports not only the music but the message of the entire service. When technical elements are off, whether it is distorted vocals, uneven levels, or feedback issues, it can hinder the ability of the music ministry to minister effectively. That's why exact, clear, and timely communication between both teams is non-negotiable.

Sound engineers must be responsive and attentive, while the music ministry must be free to follow the leading of the Holy Ghost without being burdened by technical distractions. Both teams thrive when there is mutual preparation. When plans are laid out in advance, transitions become seamless, and the worship experience is more immersive and focused.

In this kind of partnership, music is never drowned out by excessive volume or lost due to poor amplification. Instead, every voice, every instrument, and every nuance finds its place in a well-balanced sonic landscape. Excellence is not just the goal, it becomes the norm. When music and sound function in true harmony, they elevate worship from something functional to something transcendent helping the congregation engage, experience, and encounter God on a deeper level.

Your Instrument

The book of *Psalms* reveals that every instrument carries its own unique ministry. Whether it's the soaring voice of the trumpet, the solemn resonance of the organ, the sharp clarity of cymbals, or the warm tones of stringed instruments, each brings a unique timbre, a distinct musical character that defines its voice. Within that voice, pitch rises and falls, dynamics shift from soft to powerful, and expression unfolds in a way no other instrument can replicate. Likewise, the human voice as they all differ in sound.

A stringed instrument does not echo the breathy tone of a woodwind, nor does brass resemble the pulse of percussion. Some compositions are anchored by the rhythm of drums, others by the depth of piano. Some are entirely instrumental, while others are driven solely by the human voice. The more deeply we understand and master this vast musical landscape, the more powerfully and effectively we can minister through music.

As a musician, you are a steward, not only of sound but of the instrument through which that sound is made. Whether it's your voice, your body, or a physical instrument, proper care and understanding are essential. Stewardship begins with reverence: don't simply strike the drums, play them with purpose. Don't yell, sing with clarity, intention, and control. Skillful musicians understand this responsibility and model it for others.

In the end, we nurture what we value. The way we treat our instruments reflects our love, our respect for the gift, the craft, and the sacred calling behind it.

<u>Connection</u>

People are not the same every day, emotionally, mentally, or spiritually. Our internal state influences how we perceive and respond to music. A piece that stirs us deeply one day may feel distant the next. Some songs seem to resonate more in the light of morning, while others carry greater weight in the stillness of night. I once disliked a particular song, yet by the seventh year of hearing it, I had grown to love it. I've noticed slow songs can feel quicker when I'm exhausted, while upbeat tracks may seem sluggish when I'm fully alert.

These subtle, personal shifts raise important questions, especially in settings like music competitions. Judges, like all people, bring their own emotional states into the room, and their responses can be unconsciously shaped by context. A fast-paced song followed immediately by a slow one may leave a judge unprepared to adjust, potentially skewing their perception. These transitions matter. When contrasting styles or tempos are placed back-to-back without continuity, it can taint the way each piece is received, regardless of its individual quality.

The same principle applies to worship services. Through seeking God, thoughtfully choosing and arranging music isn't just about what is needed, and the mind has to be worked. You have to have variety as ministry reaches different people. It's also about creating a journey. The flow of songs helps guide the congregation emotionally and spiritually, moving them through a progression of moments that prepare their hearts for transformation. Abrupt shifts or poorly chosen sequences can interrupt that journey, creating disconnection or confusion. Because people are especially open during worship, sensitivity to the Spirit's leading is essential. The goal is never to impress, it's to foster a seamless, Spirit-led encounter that brings healing, breakthrough, and revelation.

After the word was preached at our minister's conference, a praise break followed, during which the Spirit moved powerfully, filling a sister with the Holy Ghost. The music, which had been vibrant throughout the preaching, seamlessly transitioned into a song. This song led to an eruption of praise, with the flow building from one level to the next, culminating in a spiritual breakthrough. As a result, the entire atmosphere was transformed, someone was filled with the Holy Ghost, and everyone was touched in the room.

On another occasion, the preaching and music were both intense, and as we transitioned into the altar call, we gradually slowed down, playing the song "Jesus, Jesus, Jesus" by Timothy Wright. After the altar call, we seamlessly moved into the speaker's offering, slightly increasing the tempo. The musicians then began playing "I Love You (Lord Today)," and the spirit immediately elevated the atmosphere, blessing the congregation. We maintained soft music during the announcements and benediction, then picked up the tempo after the service with "He Keeps on Doing Great Things for Me." The Spirit moved once more, and we continued for another ten minutes. The flow of the service ebbed from high energy to a more subdued pace, gradually building back up, with the Lord blessing each moment along the way.

It is not only about tempo; it also involves the weight of the song. In the weight of a song, I'm referring to its content or message, which varies according to the Spirit as God highlights what He wants for the moment. For instance, the message of the time may focus on waiting on the Lord. While praise songs are important, those that center on waiting on the Lord tend to have a deeper impact. From start to finish, the selection of music shapes the tone and flow of the service or event. The smoother the flow, the more easily the congregation connects with what is happening. Since God has created every ministry uniquely, the types of music will vary from one ministry to another. One genre does not fit all, which is why music is so versatile worldwide. Understanding the specific type of music God desires for your ministry is essential.

Even *after* the service, music continues to minister. Post-service praise or reflective worship allows people to linger in God's presence, connect with one another, and receive that final blessing before they depart. I've seen the Spirit fall during these moments, moving powerfully even after the formal conclusion. Music, when aligned with the Spirit, leads us into the next moment, even when we think the moment has passed.

Every instrument possesses a unique capacity to minister. Musicians must allow their instruments to speak in the way God intended. At times, the most powerful moment comes from silence or simplicity, a cappella voices lifting in raw, heartfelt praise. In other moments, vocalists may need to step back and allow the instrumentalists to lead, their melodies speaking the language of the Spirit. Instrumental solos, too, can carry the weight of heaven, offering praise through sound alone. Leaders must learn to feel these moments, to sense tension, momentum, and release, and shape the flow accordingly. Mastery in music ministry includes discerning when and how to move, not just what to play.

The word exhorts us to come before the Lord with singing and praise. Uplifting songs are vital for setting the tone at the start of a service or celebration. These moments invite the congregation to express joy and thanksgiving and welcome the presence of God. During prayer, however, the tone must shift, more solemn, more introspective, drawing people into reverence. In times of adversity, the church may need songs that offer encouragement, comfort, or resolve, songs about faith, endurance, the blood of Christ, and trusting in God's time. These songs carry healing power, and in altar calls, they help tenderize hearts for salvation and breakthrough.

Testimonial songs, those that speak of God's goodness and faithfulness, are also essential. They build faith and create a shared atmosphere of gratitude. There are also seasonal songs, during Christmas, Easter, or other sacred times, that help center the community around foundational truths of the faith. There is also music ministry for times when those have transitioned to the next life.

The church, like its people, moves through seasons. While there is always a place for praise, the *tone* of the music must often shift to reflect what the Spirit is doing. In seasons of grief or repentance, the songs may be subdued, meditative, or even silent. Silence, at times, becomes the most powerful sound in the room. To lead effectively, music ministers must possess not only technical skill, but deep spiritual discernment. Every note, every lyric, every transition must align with God's timing and intention.

But about that dancing...

David danced before the Lord with such abandon that it provoked the scorn of his wife, and God judged *her* for despising his praise. Miriam, the prophetess, led the women in dance, tambourine in hand, celebrating the deliverance of their people. Scripture calls us to praise Him in the dance. This is praise culture. It's what happens when a liberated spirit responds freely to the power of God. Stomping feet, clapping hands, leaping for and in joy, these are the outward signs of an inward freedom.

But let's be clear: not all movement is worship. Twerking, whining, and other suggestive forms of dance belong in the club, not the sanctuary. True praise originates in the heart. When the heart is right, the body responds in worship. Never be ashamed to praise God. Follow the Spirit, even when it feels uncomfortable or unconventional. God is not concerned with appearances, He honors authenticity.

So whether you're singing, playing, dancing, or standing in silence, do it all with excellence, with discernment, and above all, with a heart fully surrendered to Him.

God Moves His Way

In our pursuit of obedience to God, we must understand a critical truth: God does not move or think the way we do. Until we accept this, we will never live a healthy Christian life, and the music ministry, like every other form of ministry, will suffer. God operates according to His will, often in ways that defy logic and challenge our comfort zones. Many believers lose spiritual momentum simply because they cannot reconcile the seeming absurdity of God's commands with their human reasoning.

The will of God will often appear radical, even unreasonable. But if we are truly committed to worship, we must walk by faith, laying aside our own logic, embracing discomfort, and obeying God's voice, even when it carries personal cost.

Consider one of the kings of Israel. God had instructed Pharaoh to pursue the enemies of Israel. The Israelites were not to interfere. Yet, the Israelite king, believing the Israelites were inherently more worthy than the Gentiles, dismissed God's word and acted based on his own rationale. The result? He was killed in battle. Had he trusted and obeyed God, he would have lived. But because the instruction didn't make sense to him, he leaned on his own understanding and lost his life. What makes sense to God will not always make sense to us. Our responsibility is not to debate, it is to obey. We are reminded: *"Fear God and keep His commandments: for this is the whole duty of man."*

When Moses sang his song, the people recognized the movement of God and those who moved with Him lived. Those who stayed behind perished. A well-known song puts it plainly: *"When the Lord gets ready, you gotta move."*

God is not a God of tradition; He is a God of principle. Tradition, while not inherently bad, becomes dangerous when it hinders us from moving with God. Traditions are evolving practices accepted over time. Principles are eternal truths, established laws that guide change. God's principles remain constant, but they exist to initiate transformation.

The horse was once the peak of transportation; now we live in the era of space travel. The post office was once the cornerstone of communication; now, digital technology allows us to reach millions instantly. What once existed only in science fiction, video calls, voice-controlled devices, handheld computers, is now reality. These advancements didn't just happen, they occurred because God allowed them. He created space for progress so the gospel could go further, faster.

God *wants* advancement because it creates more efficient avenues for ministry. In the past, television was shunned by many Christians, viewed as a worldly distraction. But as time passed, televangelists emerged, using that same platform to preach Christ to millions. Why? Because they sensed God was shifting and changing things. They embraced the new, followed His lead, and transformed ministry in the process.

God often uses tools and methods, even people, for a season, and when the season changes, so must everything relevant. *"To everything there is a season,"* Ecclesiastes says. When one assignment concludes, God pivots, establishing something new. The mission stays the same: saving souls. But the strategy must evolve.

Take the Hammond organ, for example. Created as an affordable alternative to the pipe organ, it was once seen as a radical innovation. Yet today, it is synonymous with gospel music. Since then, musical technology has expanded exponentially: we now have advanced synthesizers, workstations, arrangers, electric drum kits, digital software, and more. We use laptops, tablets, and smartphones to produce and share music instantly. And yet, in the midst of all this innovation, we sometimes become our own worst enemies, clinging to outdated tools and resisting change out of fear or tradition.

Consider the washboard. It once served a purpose. But that season has passed. The absence of some of these things in our service to God doesn't mean we've lost reverence, it means God has moved, and we must move with Him.

God is a God of *progression*. Though He is the same yesterday, today, and forever, He leads His people forward. He has blessed us to live in modern homes, drive SUVs, connect over Wi-Fi, and worship with tools our ancestors never imagined. We no longer live in huts with dirt floors, and our ministries shouldn't either.

As each generation evolves, so must the way we minister. We cannot build meaningful, Spirit-led relationships using strategies that stopped being effective 50 years ago. If we want to be used by God in this time, we must be willing to adapt. Ministry must meet people where they are, not where they were. That includes the music we play, the tools we use, and the how we deliver the message we carry.

Music evolves because *life* evolves. And where there is no change, there is no growth.

Chapter Eight

PASS IT ON

And God said, Let the earth bring forth grass, the herb yielding seed, and the fruit tree yielding fruit after his kind, whose seed is in itself, upon the earth: and it was so. And the earth brought forth grass, and herb yielding seed after his kind, and the tree yielding fruit, whose seed was in itself, after his kind: and God saw that it was good.

Genesis 1:11-12 KJV

And these words, which I command thee this day, shall be in thine heart: And thou shalt teach them diligently unto thy children, and shalt talk of them when thou sittest in thine house, and when thou walkest by the way, and when thou liest down, and when thou risest up.

Deuteronomy 6:6-7 KJV

Hear, ye children, the instruction of a father, and attend to know understanding. For I give you good doctrine, forsake ye not my law.

Proverbs 4:1-2 KJV

Train up a child in the way he should go: and when he is old he will not depart from it.

Proverbs 22:6 KJV

<u>The Next Generation</u>

The great gift of God is life and its continuation. We cannot forget who God is or the commission He has given us. The purpose of young people in the church is to learn the ministry in order to eventually take leadership. Training is not only aimed at enhancing gifts and talents, but also at building a legacy that ensures the ongoing work of God. Leaders must be trained to be team players and people builders. They need to learn how to establish purposeful, self-sustaining, and growing organizations. It is important to cultivate young people within your local ministry because they are more likely to ensure the success of the music ministry they are familiar with. They have a vested interest in taking care of what they consider "home." The generations that follow must continue the work that has been started.

Historically, there have been generations that did not know God because the previous generation did not properly instruct the next one. A key aspect of leadership is ensuring the continuity of the organization across generations. We have the Bible today because individuals took the time to document history, some of which was autobiographical. God remains the same wonderful God, and it is essential to testify about who He is and what He has done. In sharing a testimony, we recount our personal experiences as witnesses to God's work. God has done so many great things, and it is crucial for us to remember and acknowledge His deeds.

One of my friends once told me that if they shared what God has done, people would not believe it. I believe that is precisely why they should share it. It is bewildering that we can believe in the great works of God recorded in the Bible, even though we were not there, yet we struggle to believe that God is still performing great works today, just as He did in the days of old, all around us. We often focus on teaching generational wealth, but what about generational salvation?

Transcendence

In a world full of distractions, politics, celebrity culture, personal struggles, and constant noise, it's easy to lose sight of what matters most: building and strengthening our faith that souls be saved. But if we are to minister effectively, we must learn to prioritize God's work above all else, even if that means pressing pause on everything else that demands our attention.

When our focus is divided, our ministry suffers. We risk short-circuiting our divine purpose by becoming consumed with the wrong things which is precisely what the enemy hopes for. We cannot lead others if we ourselves are led by foolishness or petty distractions.

History is filled with examples of lost generations, not because God failed, but because His ministers lost focus. As a child, it was disheartening to witness open conflict and hostility among those I once admired especially adults within the church. Those moments left an impression. Heroes are meant to inspire. They set the standard, offering a vision of what we can become when we rise above ourselves.

Music artists, whether loved or disliked, possess undeniable influence. The same is true for music ministers, musicians, and producers. Influence is embedded in the nature of their calling. And with influence comes responsibility. If we are to secure the future of the church, the next generation must clearly understand what that future should look like. We must model it for them with integrity, humility, and purpose.

Envy, jealousy, and covetousness have no place in the music ministry. Favor may not always seem fair. God chooses whom He wills, but we should be humbled that He desires to use us at all. Ministry is not a competition; it is a calling. Every opportunity to serve is a divine privilege, and we must not allow comparison to turn our eyes away from our own assignments. We shouldn't look at other ministries with distain as we all have our part.

The custodial ministry is one of the most important ministries in the church. It is a warring ministry against spirits of uncleanliness. Uncleanliness can attract evil spirits, and there are many testimonies of people encountering oppressive spirits in their homes that are accompanied by foul odors. Some individuals are trapped by certain spirits that hinder them from taking proper care of themselves, leading to poor hygiene and tattered clothing. While some may simply need assistance, others may be facing deeper spiritual struggles. Regardless of the cause, all of them need help.

This is why the house of God must reflect the holiness of the One who dwells there. Clean and spotless bathrooms, tidy kitchens, and immaculate sanctuaries matter. This isn't just about presentation, it's about reverence. We minister at a high level, and that means every detail counts. We are accountable for what we do and how we do it.

Every ministry matters. God has ordained each one for a specific purpose. Whether behind a microphone or a mop, every role contributes to the larger mission. We are co-laborers, uniquely gifted, and called to serve in unity for the glory of God.

Clean Heart

Our heart is the problem. We should all be crying out to God for this essential thing: a clean heart. A pure heart is not something we can fabricate, it must be formed in us by the hand of God. But that formation begins with surrender. We must be willing to let the Lord expose the most difficult and uncomfortable truths about ourselves. Only then can real transformation begin.

God does the cleansing, but *we* must make the choices. Ask yourself: *Do you truly want to be saved?* And if you are already saved, *do you truly want to stay that way?*

For those who believe that salvation is eternally secure the moment one is born again, consider this: there were once beings who lived in the very presence of God, yet they were cast out. Lucifer and his followers were not the only ones to rebel in heaven. Let that sink in. If rebellion could occur there, how much more must we guard our hearts here?

Do not be swayed by modern philosophies or cultural ideologies. Just because something sounds wise or resonates with emotion does not mean it is true. Many ideas are simply creative reasoning, clever, but hollow. Opinion may be subjective. Morality may shift with culture. But truth real truth is eternal. It is unchanging. It applies to everyone.

Training

Fall in love with the process of addressing problems, not just finding answers. True leadership isn't about rushing to quick fixes; it's about learning to sit with the problem long enough to understand its roots. Surface-level issues are easy to identify, but real growth comes from uncovering what lies beneath.

I noticed that some of the young people were eager to be involved in the music ministry. But to secure their long-term commitment, I realized they had to feel a sense of ownership. That meant I needed to go deeper beneath the surface excitement to understand the dynamics shaping their interest, motivation, and engagement. It was only by addressing the real issues that I could build meaningful solutions and offer them the tools they truly needed.

When training others, don't just hand them tools, teach them how to use them. Then, step back. Allow them to explore, test, and discover. Don't correct them unless their efforts are causing harm. Instead, encourage experimentation. At some point, healthy detachment becomes necessary; they must learn to navigate challenges without always leaning on you. When they grasp the essentials and begin applying their own creativity, it's time to remove the safety nets and let them grow.

When working with young people, obedience must be framed as a standard, not a suggestion. They must be taught to honor their parents, not just as a rule, but as a foundational value of godly living. Ministry is leadership and effective leaders must lead by example. No one is truly qualified to serve before God without adhering to His principles including children. Children are a gift from God, but they require teaching. Discipline, when done in love, is not punishment it is preparation. God disciplines those He loves. So we must consistently teach, nurture, and guide them in God's truth especially in understanding the purpose, responsibility, and spiritual weight of the music ministry.

Being gifted is a blessing but talent without discipline holds little weight in God's kingdom. Without the ability to submit to spiritual authority and God's Word, even the most gifted person becomes a liability. Authority is not oppression, it's protection. Independence that is rooted in pride leads to spiritual stagnation. But those who embrace teamwork, humility, and shared vision help build a ministry that thrives.

The music ministry should never be a source of division or drama. But when people lack self-control and humility, that's exactly what it becomes. Unity is fragile and it is sustained only when every member understands that ministry is not about individual expression, but collective engagement.

The music ministry is one of joy. People love to sing, celebrate, and feel moved. But they also want to feel seen and valued. They want to connect with what they're apart of. So pay attention, discover what resonates with your fellow music ministers and congregation. Don't just speak to it, respond to it through action, leadership, and love.

Above all, remain obedient to God's will. Building a successful ministry requires more than talent. It requires prayer, fasting, and unwavering dedication. It's not easy work but it is holy work.

God's Music Ministry

When God calls us to a task, our response must be both immediate and deliberate. We are not called to stumble blindly into service. We are called to prepare, to learn, and to position ourselves to be used effectively for His glory. We owe God not just our time or talent, but our very best, our whole selves.

To build the kind of music ministry that honors God, we must go beyond surface-level engagement. We must study its purpose, discern His expectations, learn how to execute with excellence, and be equipped to teach and guide others. This level of ministry demands dedication, spiritual insight, and humility.

Now is the time to surrender our own agendas and embrace God's vision. This is God's music ministry. Everything belongs to Him, the music, the message, and the mission. He alone knows what is truly needed to accomplish His work.

Submit to the overseer God has placed in your life, and seek the mind of God with diligence. Reject sin. Set yourself apart. Commit fully to the service of the Lord. Through the word of God, prayer, fasting, and sanctification, you will be transformed and so will the music ministry around you.

And when you fully align with God's will, you will witness Him move in ways so powerful, so undeniable, that you would scarcely believe it if it hadn't happened to you.

May God bless you and your music ministry. I sincerely pray for your success, and I hope you have received a great blessing from this publication. It is truly a great and wonderful honor, to be in God's service.

Selah.

About the Author

James Edward Goodlett

I have devoted my life to serving God through music ministry, church leadership, and community outreach. From 1994 to 2009, I served as the Minister of Music at Christ Holiness Apostolic Temple in Cedar Rapids Iowa, where I was responsible for developing and leading music ministries, training choirs, musicians, and vocalists. I also held the position of Minister of Music for the Missouri Council during the Jesus Christ Apostolic Churches Inc. (JCAC) era and served as Youth Director for Christ Apostolic Temple Fellowship Inc. from 2006 to 2011. Throughout these years, I led rehearsals, composed and produced original music for choirs, television, and podcasts, and many times served as the sole musician at church functions across the country. From 2015-2025 I was the band leader at Christ Apostolic Temple in Des Moines Iowa.

I have organized and directed numerous music programs, working to demonstrate strong leadership in both performance and spiritual formation. In addition to my musical responsibilities, I was privileged to assist in planting churches in Cedar Rapids Iowa, Knoxville Iowa, Louisville Kentucky, and Racine Wisconsin. These efforts included evangelism, canvassing, door-to-door outreach, and transporting people to services. I frequently traveled on weekends to support these works, providing both musical and spiritual support.

I began my ministerial service at the founding of a church in Hannibal, MO, and since then have carried out a wide range of ministerial duties. I have done weddings, visited the sick and elderly, ministered in nursing homes, worked on altar teams, and participated in baptisms and tarrying services. I have, taught Sunday school, taught bible classes, and preached Sunday morning messages. My service has extended into technical and operational roles as well, including managing the church's sound department, cooking for congregational events, maintaining the facilities, and supporting the financial operations of the church. While fulfilling these responsibilities, I have also balanced family life and employment-sometimes working three jobs at once-always trusting that the work done for God is not in vain.

Now I am the husband of the pastor of the church in Racine Wisconsin, Aisha Goodlett, continuing a lifelong commitment to ministry. My passion for God's work is unwavering, and I am profoundly grateful for the guidance I've received from Bishop Jeremiah Reed, Mother Willie Mae Reed, Bishop Dwight A. Reed, my mother Tonya Oliver-McGregor, my brother Ismail Oliver, and my wife, Pastor Aisha Goodlett. Their leadership and support have helped shape my understanding of what true music ministry is. Church has never been a part-time endeavor for me. It has been my life's calling. Through every season, I remain committed to glorifying God through service, leadership, and the transformative power of music.

www.ingramcontent.com/pod-product-compliance
Lightning Source LLC
Chambersburg PA
CBHW071310130626
46556CB00004B/1555